EMPLOYMENT AND
ECONOMIC GROWTH
IN URBAN CHINA
1949–1957

Morning light in the Shanghai suburbs

Employment
and economic growth
in urban China
1949–1957

CHRISTOPHER HOWE

CAMBRIDGE

at the University Press 1971

Published by the Syndics of the Cambridge University Press
Bentley House, 200 Euston Road, London N.W.1
American Branch: 32 East 57th Street, New York, N.Y.10022

© Cambridge University Press 1971

Library of Congress Catalogue Card Number: 76–152641

ISBN: 0 521 08172 6

Printed in Great Britain by
Alden & Mowbray Ltd at the Alden Press, Oxford

1607332

For my family

The positive functions of the city cannot be performed without creating new institutional arrangements, capable of coping with the vast energies modern man now commands: arrangements just as bold as those that originally transformed the overgrown village and its stronghold into the nucleated, highly organized city.

Lewis Mumford, *The City in History*

CONTENTS

Frontispiece: Morning light in the Shanghai suburbs, from *Photographs of the new Shanghai* (Shanghai People's Art Publishing House, 1965)

List of diagrams	*page* ix
List of tables	ix
Preface	xi
Chronology of important political, economic and employment events, 1949–58	xiii
Abbreviations	xvii
A note on romanisation	xix
Introduction	1

PART ONE: ECONOMIC DEVELOPMENT AND EMPLOYMENT CHANGE IN URBAN AREAS

1	The development of the urban economy	9
2	The growth and structure of the urban labour force	29
3	The determinants of structural employment change	49
4	Employment fluctuations and their consequences	74

PART TWO: EMPLOYMENT POLICY AND ADMINISTRATION

5	The foundation of the Labour Bureaux and the beginnings of employment administration, 1949–52	87
6	First steps in employment planning, 1953–55	102
7	High tide, crisis and reform, 1956–57	118
8	The aftermath of central planning	138

Appendix: Sources for the estimate of the structure of non-agricultural employment in Shanghai, 1957	152
Bibliography	156
Indexes	167

DIAGRAMS

1 Industrial production: annual percentage changes 1950–57 *page* 15
2 Industrial production in Shanghai: annual percentage changes
  1950–57   15
3 Retail sales: annual percentage changes 1951–57 (urban
  and rural sales)   16
4 Index of urban population growth 1949–57   16
5 Inflow and outflow from the Higher Middle School system:
  the situation in 1957   125

TABLES

1 Indexes of industrial production (national), 1949–57 *page* 12
2 Index of industrial production for Shanghai, 1949–57   12
3 Index of retail sales (urban and rural areas), 1950–57   13
4 Index of output of private industry (national), 1949–55   13
5 The share of the private sector in total industrial output,
  1949–55   13
6 Annual percentage changes in the level of private sector
  industrial output in Shanghai, 1951–53   13
7 The share of the private sector in Shanghai industrial output,
  1949–55   14
8 Employment in industry, 1949–57   14
9 Employment in the construction industry, 1949–57   14
10 The share of the private sector in retail sales, 1950–57   14
11 The population of Shanghai, 1949–65 (urban and rural)   34
12 A summary of population movements into and out of
   Shanghai, 1949–57   35
13 Categories of emigrants from Shanghai, 1949–57   36
14 Emigration from Shanghai, 1949–57   37

TABLES

15 The supply of job seekers and the supply of non-agricultural employment in Shanghai, 1949–57   39

16 The structure of employment in Shanghai in 1957   40

17 The structure of employment in Shanghai by main sectors in 1957   41

18 The structure of non-agricultural employment in Shanghai by traditional and modern sectors in 1957   41

19 The structure of employment in Shanghai by main sectors: 1926/27 and 1957   42

20 The employed population as a percentage of total population: national, Shanghai and other cities, pre-1937 and the late 1950s   44

21 Growth rates of population and workers and staff, 1949–57   47

22 Indexes of industrial output, labour, capital, 1952–57 (national)   52

23 Growth rates of industrial output, labour, capital and productivity, 1952–57 (national)   53

24 Growth rates of industrial output, labour, capital and productivity in Shanghai city and Kansu Province, 1952–57   54

25 The growth of industrial output, employment and capital in Shanghai, 1933–57   56

26 Industrial employment as a percentage of total employment and population in Shanghai, Canton, Peking and all urban areas, 1931–57   57

27 The age structure of workers and employees in public sector industry and capital construction in 1955   61

28 The age structure of workers in a Shanghai textile mill in the late 1920s   62

29 Females as a percentage of the total employed labour force in Shanghai in 1957   63

30 Females and children as a percentage of the factory labour force in Shanghai, 1931–57   63

31 Employment fluctuations: national and local data, 1949–57   75

32 Numbers of registered unemployed in all urban areas, East China and Shanghai, 1950–51   95

PREFACE

This study is a result of the development of economic studies at the School of Oriental and African Studies, London, and I have benefited in many ways from working with colleagues in the Department of Politics and Economics. In particular I wish to thank Professor Edith Penrose, who as head of the department gave early support to my research plans, and Dr Kenneth Walker. Dr Walker first suggested to me that China's labour problems would be worth investigating, and in the past seven years he has provided a continuous supply of encouragement and detailed advice on sources and the problems involved in trying to understand and explain the Chinese economy. I am also grateful to Mr Peter Ayre who read an early version of Chapter 1 and Dr William Warren with whom I have had many useful discussions on the labour problems of low income countries.

Like all scholars in this field I am indebted to courteous and learned librarians in Asia, Europe and America. In Hong Kong, the staffs of the Union Research Institute and the Universities Service Centre helped to make research there an exciting and pleasurable activity. In Tokyo, the director of the Tōyō Bunko and Professor Ishikawa Shigeru enabled me to make far more efficient use of my time in the great Japanese collections of Chinese sources than would otherwise have been possible.

For the early years of the journal of the Chinese Ministry of Labour I am grateful to the staffs of the School and the Lenin Library Moscow. Later issues of the same journal were supplied to me by Mr John Philip Emerson of the U.S. Bureau of the Census, who has always taken a friendly and expert interest in my research.

I should like to acknowledge generous travel grants from the Committee on the Economy of China of the Social Science Research Council, New York and the London Committee of the London–Cornell Project.

Some of the materials in Chapter 2 were incorporated in a paper read at the conference on Economic Organisation in Chinese Society, Ste-Adèle-en-haut, Canada, sponsored by the Social Science Research Council, New York and the American Council of Learned Societies. I am grateful both to the discussants, Professor Albert Feuerwerker and Professor William G. Skinner, and to others at the conference who made suggestions that were subsequently used in this chapter.

Mrs Anthony Dicks produced a readable manuscript from most unpromising materials and I am grateful to Professor Stuart Schram, Mr David Wilson and the Contemporary China Insitute, for providing financial and editorial solutions to many of the problems that beset authors in the final stages of book presentation.

My wife, Patricia Howe, rescued the manuscript from abandonment on several occasions and also helped me to eliminate some of its grosser errors of grammar and presentation.

CHRISTOPHER HOWE

London
October 1970

CHRONOLOGY OF IMPORTANT POLITICAL, ECONOMIC AND EMPLOYMENT EVENTS, 1949–58

1949 August   publication in Shanghai of *methods for the resolution of disputes relating to the restoration of output and employment*.

       October   The Central People's Government established.

1950 May   publication of directives on *the establishment of Labour Bureaux at the provincial and municipal levels*.

         publication of a directive on *the organization of labour introduction offices*.

         publication of *methods for the registration and placing of unemployed skilled workers*.

       June   publication of directives on *the relief of unemployed workers*.

       November   China enters the Korean War.

1951 February   publication of *labour insurance regulations* (including retirement rules).

       May   publication of *regulations governing hiring of workers and staff in all areas*.

       August   Shanghai labour market begins to tighten.

       September/
       October   local and national reports of full capacity being reached in many sectors.

       November   the *san fan* movement begins (directed against waste and bureaucratic corruption).

1952 February/
       May   the *wu fan* movement begins (directed against the power of the private economic sector in the cities).

       June/
       September   measures to revive the urban economy after its collapse in the *wu fan*.

	July	publication of the *decisions on the problem of employment*.
1953	January	the *First Five Year Plan* period begins.
		publication of the *revised regulations for labour insurance* (and retirement).
	July	Korean armistice.
	August	publication of *decisions on the strengthening of labour discipline*.
1954	February	campaign to reduce the power of the private sector and to speed urban socialisation.
	July	publication of the *model outline of intra-enterprise disciplinary rules*.
1955	Spring	campaign to reduce the size of the urban population (*hsia fang*).
	July	major political purge begins.
	October	publication of Mao's call for accelerated agricultural cooperativisation.
	December	publication of new *retirement regulations for employees in state organisations*.
	December/ Spring 1956	the cooperativisation drive in rural areas.
1956	January	the socialisation of urban industry, commerce and handicrafts.
		publication of the *Twelve Year Plan for Agriculture*.
	June	the wage reform.
	September	First draft of *Second Five Year Plan*.
1957	February	Mao speaks on '*Contradictions*'.
	June	rectification campaign begins to correct the errors of the 'Hundred Flowers' campaign and to secure increased responsiveness in the Party, bureaucracy and people.
	July	publication of *regulations on the treatment of workers and staff subject to inter-enterprise reallocation*.
	August	new *hsia fang* movement to encourage participation by cadres in physical labour and to send cadres and surplus population to the countryside.
	October	discussions on the *Second Five Year Plan*.

	November	publication of the *revised retirement regulations for all workers and staff.*
	December	the *First Five Year Plan* ends.
		publication of the *regulations governing the recruitment of temporary labour from the countryside.*
1958	February	publication of *regulations governing visits by urban workers to their families.*
	September	publication of *directives on the reform of the planning system.*

ABBREVIATIONS

CCCP	Ching chi chou pao
CCHHJP	Chung ch'ing hsin hua jih pao
CCJP	Ch'ang chiang jih pao
CFJP	Chieh fang jih pao
CHCC	Chi hua ching chi
CHJP	Ch'ing hai jih pao
CKCNP	Chung kuo ch'ing nien pao
CLJP	Chi lin jih pao
CSCS	Ch'eng shih chien she
FCJP	Fu chien jih pao
HCS	Hsin chien she
HEPJP	Ha erh pin jih pao
HH	Hsüh hsi
HHPYK	Hsin hua pan yüeh k'an
HHYP	Hsin hua yüeh pao
HLCJP	Hei lung chiang jih pao
HWJP	Hsin wen jih pao
JMJP	Jen min jih pao
KCJP	Kuang chou jih pao
KJJP	Kung jen jih pao
KMJP	Kuang ming jih pao
KSJP	Kan su jih pao
LNJP	Liao ning jih pao
LT	Lao tung
NCNA	New China News Agency
NFJP	Nan fang jih pao
NMKJP	Nei meng ku jih pao
SCMP	Survey of the China Mainland Press
SHJP	Shan hsi jih pao
SHYK	She hui yüeh k'an
STJP	Shan t'ou jih pao

ABBREVIATIONS

SYJP	*Shen yang jih pao*
TCJP	*T'ien chin jih pao*
TCKT	*T'ung chi kung tso*
TKP	*Ta kung pao*
TPJP	*Tung pei jih pao*
WHP	*Wen hui pao*

A NOTE ON ROMANISATION

The system followed in this book is the modified Wade–Giles system as used in C. H. Fenn's *The five thousand dictionary*. Place names follow standard usage, and for bibliographical consistency Chinese personal names are cited with the surname first, as in Chinese practice.

INTRODUCTION

This book is a study of China's urban employment problems set in the context of growth and fluctuations in the urban economy between 1949 and 1957. Its main objectives are to analyse the size and determinants of urban employment change, and to trace the evolution both of Chinese thinking about employment and the institutions of labour control that reflected this thinking in day-to-day administration.

The study is focused mainly on the period 1949–57 for two reasons. The first is that data after 1957 become scarce in quantity and obscure in meaning. Analysis that attempts to span the pre- and post-1957 periods therefore involves discontinuities in method. More important, the years before 1958 constitute a period of relatively self-contained significance. During these years the Government extended their control over the economy by means of a series of radical institutional transformations; so that, although the objectives of economic policy remained basically stable, an astonishing variety of techniques were experimented with in pursuit of their achievement. Thus during these years the Government acquired an understanding of the whole range of economic problems that confronted them, and also experience of the implications of alternative strategies for solving them.

In a considerable number of ways the Great Leap Forward marked the high point of this process of experimentation, and it is improbable that the extremities of institutional reform, resource mobilisation and grass roots utopianism found in China in the summer of 1958 have been or will be exceeded. Certainly the upheavals of the Cultural Revolution, which has many superficial similarities with the Leap, do not appear to have been accompanied by radical economic change.

The problems of employment policy and administration formed only a part of the economic preoccupations of the Government

during these years; and for most of the period, employment considerations were only secondary to other more basic objectives. The
achievement of these objectives, however, proved more dependent on
correct labour policies than the Chinese had expected. At the peaks
and troughs of activity one can generally see the operations of the
labour market with exceptional clarity, and one can see the way in
which employment considerations assumed critical importance. For
this reason we have tried to analyse labour issues in the context of
the overall management of the economy.

In putting employment policy into the context of overall economic
management, we have tried particularly hard to understand the
character of short term economic planning and the actual workings
of labour administration. Economists have spent much time analysing structural economic change and the formal administrative
machinery of socialist economies and it is proper that they should
have done so; but there remains the danger that we shall lose sight
of the fact that even the planners and administrators of socialist
economies are profoundly affected by their working environment of
unpredictable external shocks; lack of administrative personnel;
and perpetually shifting political constraints. Anyone who has
studied China's economic administration in detail becomes aware
that even at the highest levels a great deal of attention is concentrated on the problems of year to year, quarter to quarter and, at
times, even day-to-day management. Studying the problems of
planning and administration from this perspective enables one to
understand something of the complex character of the relationships
between different aspects of Chinese economic policy and to link
these changes with the wider, political landscape. One can also see
the way in which cumulative experience has sometimes led to an
almost spontaneous generation of radical new policies; thus actions
that might have been interpreted in terms of ideological dogmatism
or the whims of a dictator, can suddenly appear as the outcome of
logical, but scarcely visible processes.

The materials that we have used are partly materials familiar to
scholars who have worked on Chinese labour problems; the bulk of
our data, however, have been drawn from Chinese materials that
hitherto have not been subject to any systematic analysis, and for the

most part have not even been looked at. Two sources have been particularly important: the Journal of the Ministry of Labour *Lao tung* (Labour) 1950–64; and the four Shanghai daily newspapers which together with the Shanghai journal *Ching chi chou pao* (The economic weekly) 1950–54, have enabled us to build up a detailed picture of employment change and economic administration in Shanghai. This picture has been used to supplement and where possible improve upon the analysis of the national data. We have also used the files of the Union Research Institute (Hong Kong) and the holdings of the Library of Congress to obtain local newspaper material for other cities, in particular Canton, Lanchow and the larger Manchurian cities.

In our view these local materials provide a more satisfactory approach to the understanding of the Chinese economy than highly aggregated, national data. Information at the local level is often available in detail that enables one to answer more complex and economically more interesting questions than is possible with national data. More important, both the variety of China's resource endowment and the discriminatory character of economic development policies in the First Five Year Plan suggest that the process of economic growth and the character of economic problems may be subject to variations so significant that crude aggregation may leave one with a picture that is false and at times even incomprehensible. The findings of this study give support to this view.

A further reason for the study of individual cities is that through them it is sometimes possible to bridge the pre- and post-1949 periods. National statistics for the pre-war period are either non-existent or guesswork, and this is unfortunate for those who consider that evaluation of the post-1949 economic performance must depend in some degree on an understanding of the pre-war period. The data for individual cities is often better than guesswork. The pre-war data for Shanghai for example, while they leave much to be desired, are sufficient for us to draw some important and at times unexpected comparisons with the later period.

We had hoped that it might prove possible to construct a detailed picture of the economy of several cities, but this proved over-

3

ambitious and it therefore seemed worthwhile to concentrate on one city – Shanghai – and to supplement this with incomplete information on other cities where it seemed appropriate to do so. In particular we have attempted to analyse the growth of urban Kansu, a province which offers striking contrasts with Shanghai.

Shanghai is attractive for several reasons. First, there is the exceptional availability of materials containing usable data. Secondly, it seems probable that Shanghai statistical materials have an accuracy above average even for urban areas. In the pre-war period the Shanghai Municipal Government acquired considerable experience in statistical work, and under it the Bureau of Social Affairs undertook a number of pioneering studies which included surveys of the city's labour force and economic structure.[1] This experience, together with the above average literacy and sophistication still evident in the city, gives one a measure of confidence in any data produced by the city authorities.[2] We cannot of course argue that a local approach to measurement problems produces any certain conclusions, but it has proved possible to reconstitute a mass of qualitative and quantitative information into a picture that is internally consistent and economically meaningful.

Any study of Shanghai is of interest in its own right. The city is the largest in China and in 1957 still accounted for 7% of China's urban population and about 20% of all industrial production. The scale of Shanghai as an economic unit is indicated by the fact that by the mid-1960s its population (including the rural suburbs under the city's administration) was larger than sixty of the eighty-three underdeveloped countries listed by the Association for International Development.[3] In terms of agricultural and industrial output and the generation of technical and organisational skills, it is probable that Shanghai's ranking would be even higher in this list.

It is however important to appreciate that the relative economic

[1] The results of five industrial surveys are given in, D.K. Lieu, *The growth and industrialization of Shanghai* (1936). In addition, the Bureau of Social Affairs produced fourteen surveys of labour conditions between 1918 and 1947.

[2] When the present writer visited Shanghai briefly in 1965 and 1966 he was struck by the evident competence of local administrators and the high level of educational activity in the city.

[3] John Pincus, *Trade, aid and development: the rich and the poor nations* (1967), pp. 69–71.

4

maturity of the city in 1949 and its historically determined peculiarities of economic structure, imply that generalisations about urban China based on the study of this particular city have to be made with great care. But having said this, we can point out that the development of the city *after* 1949, whether considered in terms of demographic, employment or industrial change, was in fact similar to that of other cities which, like Shanghai, were *not* designated as 'key points' for rapid growth.

The plan of the book is as follows. In Chapter 1 we sketch the urban economic environment in terms of population, employment, output and the evolution of the instruments of economic control. In Chapter 2 we explore the dimensions of urban employment change and Chapters 3 and 4 use these data as a basis for analysing employment trends and the significance of employment fluctuations. In Chapters 5 to 7 the findings of the earlier chapters are used as the setting for an account of the evolution of employment policy and administration.

In Chapter 8 we summarise our conclusions and relate these both to our broader understanding of economic change in China in the 1950s and to our knowledge of trends in employment administration in the early 1960s.

In conclusion, we must stress that this study is largely an experimental work that explores only some aspects of an enormous problem and utilises only a fraction of the materials available to scholars interested in understanding China's cities. In particular, we have not pursued the problem of wage determination and its relationship to employment issues as far as we should have liked. We intend to examine wage problems in a later monograph and hope that even with these limitations, we have been able to suggest some unfamiliar dimensions to China's recent economic history. If this book succeeds in stimulating others to pick up some of its loose threads and weave them into a more systematic and close knit fabric, the time spent on it will have been worthwhile.

PART ONE

ECONOMIC DEVELOPMENT AND EMPLOYMENT CHANGE IN URBAN AREAS

I

THE DEVELOPMENT OF THE URBAN ECONOMY

THE URBAN ECONOMY BEFORE 1949

When the transfer of power took place in 1949 the urban economy was in a state of collapse. The population of the cities was swollen by refugees; industrial production and most other economic activities were far below pre-war peaks; unemployment was high and inflation and food shortages which were evident reflected both a collapse of administration and major structural dislocations in production caused by almost twenty years of continuous warfare.[1]

Before 1949 the location, pace and character of urban development in modern China had been determined predominantly by external forces. The growth of population and economic activity in the cities of the southern and eastern seaboard had been stimulated by the Western Powers who, in the nineteenth and early twentieth century, had established the Treaty Port system. After 1931 the growth and industrialisation of the Manchurian cities had been accelerated by the Japanese. As a result of these stimuli, the urban population in the pre-communist period was growing at moderate rates, and by 1949 the urban population was about 58,000,000 – 11% of the total population.[2] Thus although the rural population remained overwhelmingly predominant, in absolute terms China already had an urban population of enormous size.

The economic base that supported this population was however both slight and structurally defective; for although industrial output

[1] A graphic account of the economic problems of the takeover is given by Ch'en Yün, 'Conquer financial difficulties; achieve price stability', *Chieh fang jih pao* (Liberation daily, hereafter *CFJP*) 5 Dec. 1949; also 'The work report of the East China Military Government', *CFJP* 4 Feb. 50.

[2] Shanghai, for example, grew at 4·8% per annum between 1890 and 1930; Tientsin at 4·2% per annum between 1900 and 1935, see: Rhoads Murphy, *Shanghai: key to modern China* (1953), ch. 2; H.O. Kung, 'The growth of population of the six large Chinese cities', in *Chinese economic journal and bulletin*, Mar. 1937, pp. 301–14.

9

had been growing at an average rate of 5·5% since before the First World War, industry remained insignificant in absolute terms and highly dependent on external economic relations for its continued and efficient functioning. Per capita outputs of such commodities as steel, electricity and cotton are quantitative indicators that confirm the smallness of the industrial base. These all suggest that levels of output in China were not only low by comparison with those of advanced countries, but even by comparison with the Soviet Union in 1928.[1]

Economic backwardness was also reflected in the structure of urban employment as well as in the character of labour force participation and labour market mechanisms. The main feature of the structure of employment was that modern industry accounted for only about one million persons, which was probably less than 5% of total urban employment.[2] The rest of the work force was engaged in modern services or in the traditional handicrafts, service, trading and transportation sectors.

Surveys suggest that overall, a fairly high proportion of the population had some gainful form of occupation, but that there were marked variations in hours worked. In the factory sector twelve-hour and longer working days were common, but in traditional trades employment was often casual and subject to sharp seasonal variations. There were also periodic crises of open unemployment related to foreign trade and domestic agriculture.[3]

Hiring procedures in pre-1949 China were characterised by the importance of guilds and job broking networks and by a general preference for hiring through personal contact and assessment, rather than through public advertisement and the application of objective criteria of suitability.

---

[1] The rate of growth of output is an estimate by John K. Chang, 'Industrial development of mainland China 1912–1949', *The journal of economic history*, XXVII, Mar. 1967. A useful survey of the absolute size of the Chinese industrial base in 1949 is in W. W. Rostow, *The prospects for Communist China*, (1954), ch. 12.

[2] See discussion in Chapters 2 and 3.

[3] The quality of pre-war materials on the urban work force is not uniform, but some usable information is available. See for example the materials in yearbooks quoted in the bibliography. Statistical information on the Shanghai labour force in the 1930s is contained in *Statistics of Shanghai compiled in 1933* (1933). An important survey of the factory labour force in the late 1940s is, *Shang hai kung ch'ang lao kung t'ung chi* (Statistics of Shanghai's factory labour), (1947).

Thus, in sum we would argue that the size, structure and organisational characteristics of the economic base for the new cities of socialist China, were inadequate for the requirements of the new leadership. For although the rural roots of the Chinese Communist Party were too deep for it ever to share the classical Marxist contempt for the 'idiocy' of rural life, in 1949 the Party shifted its centre of interest decisively to the urban areas, and expected that these would provide the material, technological and organisational means not only for their own economic and social transformation, but for the socialisation of the countryside also. Thus whereas in Western Europe and America the urbanisation of society had been accomplished by the bourgeoisie, in China (as in Russia), this work was to become part of the historic mission of the proletariat.[1]

ECONOMIC GROWTH AND FLUCTUATIONS 1949–57

Let us now consider some of the main indicators of economic growth and fluctuations in the urban economy. Tables 1 to 10 and Diagrams 1 to 4 below present data on population, industrial output, retail sales and the construction and private industrial sectors.

All the indicators suggest rapid growth. Industrial production grew at rates between 20·4% per annum and 23·8% per annum according to one's choice of index. Industrial employment grew at 12·6% per annum while the urban population increased from 58 millions to almost 100 millions – equal to 15% of total population and included fourteen cities with more than a million inhabitants, a greater number than in any other country. The absolute size of the industrial economy had also grown significantly although industrial employment was still small in relation to total population and work force.[2]

The other interesting feature of these tables is the fluctuations that they reveal. Fluctuations are apparent in the aggregate industrial

[1] Karl Marx and Frederick Engels, *Manifesto of the Communist Party* in *Selected Works*, I, p. 238 (1962); Hua Kang, 'A discussion of the law of the development of relations between town and country', *Hsin hua chou pao* (New China Weekly) Vol. 4, No. 6, 14 Jan. 1950, pp. 8–9.
[2] See Table 26, Chapter 3.

Table 1. *Indexes of industrial production (national), 1949–57*

		1949	1950	1951	1952	1953	1954	1955	1956	1957
	a	100	136	188	245	319	370	391	502	559
% change			+36	+38	+30	+30	+16	+6	+28	+11
	b	100	133	189	244	299	348	361	459	504
% change			+33	+42	+29	+23	+16	+4	+27	+10
	c	100	130	174	226	282	320	332	410	442
% change			+30	+34	+30	+25	+13	+4	+23	+8

SOURCES:
[a] Official index of the gross value of production of industry (modern and workshop), *Ten great years* (1960), p. 87.
[b] A reconstructed index by Michael Field in Joint Economic Committee Congress of the United States, *An economic profile of Mainland China* (hereafter *The profile*), (1967), I, p. 273.
[c] An index of factory production by Chao Kang, *The rate and pattern of industrial growth in Communist China* (1965), p. 88.

Table 2. *Index of industrial production for Shanghai, 1949–57*

	1949	1950	1951	1952	1953	1954	1955	1956	1957
	100	102	160	195	263	282	269	371	379
Annual % change		+2	+56	+22	+35	+7	−5	+38	+2

This is an index of gross value of output based on scattered official data and excludes handicraft production. There are many sources which contain data on changes in aggregate Shanghai industrial production and among these there are slight variations. In choosing sources, we have in general preferred those which contained a short series of data rather than individual figures. It is very difficult to appraise the accuracy of this official index since we lack the data necessary to construct a comprehensive index of our own. However, it may be noted that at one point in our research, when we had no official index numbers for 1950 and 1951, estimates for those years based on production data for individual industries subsequently proved to be within 2% of the official estimates for both years.

SOURCES:
'The achievements of economic and finance work in Shanghai during the past five years', *Hsin Hua yüeh pao* (New China monthly, hereafter *HHYP*) 1955 No. 4, pp. 96–9; 'Rationally develop public utility enterprises so that they are more useful both to industry and citizens', *CFJP* 21 Aug. 1956; 'Report on the implementation of the 1956 national plan in Shanghai and the plan for 1957', *Hsin wen jih pao* (The daily news, hereafter *HWJP*) 28 Aug. 1957. 'Total output doubled in five years', *HWJP* 28 Dec. 1957.

Table 3. *Index of retail sales (urban and rural areas), 1950–57*

	1950	1951	1952	1953	1954	1955	1956	1957
% change	100	137	162	204	223	229	270	278
		+37	+18	+26	+9	+3	+18	+3

SOURCE: *Ten great years*, p. 166.

Table 4. *Index of output of private industry (national), 1949–55*

	1949	1950	1951	1952	1953	1954	1955
% change	100	107	148	154	195	152	106
		+7	+39	+4	+24	−22	−30

SOURCE: Ch'ien Hua *et al.*, *Ch'i nien lai wo kuo szu ying kung shang yeh ti pien hua* (The transformation in private industry and commerce in our country during the past seven years), (1957), p. 8.

Table 5. *The share of the private sector in total industrial output, 1949–55*

(%)						
1949	1950	1951	1952	1953	1954	1955
65·3	54·7	54·1	44·0	42·5	37·2	32·3

SOURCE: *Ten great years*, p. 38.

Table 6. *Annual percentage changes in the level of private sector industrial output in Shanghai, 1951–53*

			1951	1952	1953
% change	–	–	+63	−4	+34

SOURCES: 'The reform of Shanghai's private industry during the past four years', *Jen min jih pao* (The people's daily, hereafter *JMJP*) 3 Mar. 1954; 'Shanghai industry helps national construction', *Wen hui pao* (The cultural contact daily, hereafter *WHP*) 27 Aug. 1954.

C

Table 7. *The share of the private sector in Shanghai industrial output,*
1949–55

(%)						
1949	1950	1951	1952	1953	1954	1955
83[a]	83[b]	87[c]	68[d]	63[e]	n.a.	35[f]

SOURCES:
[a] and [f] 'Mobilise every energy and actively utilise Shanghai's industrial potential',
HWJP 8 Aug. 1956.
[b, c, d] estimates based on the assumption that the private sector's share did not fall in
1950 and on data referred to in Tables 2 and 6.
[e] 'Shanghai statistical bureau report on the implementation of the 1953 state plan
in Shanghai', *WHP* 20 Sep. 1954.

Table 8. *Employment in industry, 1949–57*

	(millions)								
	1949	1950	1951	1952	1953	1954	1955	1956	1957
	3·059	3·386	4·379	5·263	6·121	6·370	6·121	7·480	7·907
% change		+11	+29	+20	+16	+4	−4	+22	+6

SOURCE: John Philip Emerson, *Nonagricultural employment in mainland China: 1949–*
1957 (1965), Table 1, p. 128.

Table 9. *Employment in the construction industry, 1949–57*

	1949	1950	1951	1952	1953	1954	1955	1956	1957
	0·200	0·400	0·600	1·048	2·170	2·100	1·935	2·951	1·910
% change		+100	+50	+75	+107	−3	−8	+53	−35

SOURCE: Emerson (1965), Table 1, p. 128.

Table 10. *The share of the private sector in retail sales, 1950–57*

(%)							
1950	1951	1952	1953	1954	1955	1956	1957
85	75·5	57·2	49·9	25·6	17·8	4·2	2·7

SOURCE: *Ten great years*, p. 40.

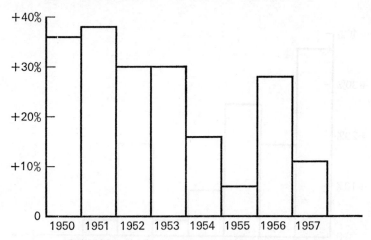

1. Industrial production: annual percentage changes 1950–57.
    Source: Table 1, note *a*

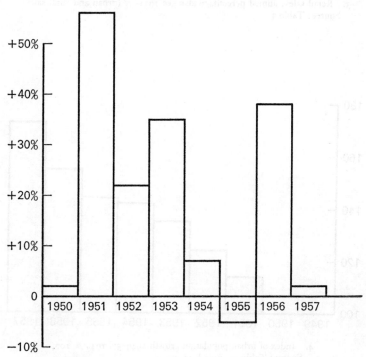

2. Industrial production in Shanghai: annual percentage changes 1950–57.
    Source: Table 2

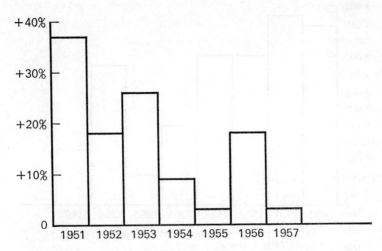

3. Retail sales: annual percentage changes 1951–57 (urban and rural sales).
Source: Table 3

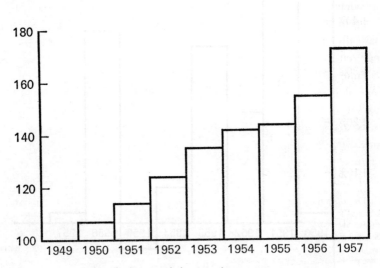

4. Index of urban population growth 1949–57. 1949 = 100.
Source: Table 21, note 1, p. 47

production and employment data, but a degree of sectoral and geographical disaggregation adds extremely interesting dimensions to the picture. The crucial sectoral data are those for private industrial output and total construction activity (using employment data as an indicator of the latter). These are shown in Tables 4 and 9. A geographical disaggregation is provided by total and private industrial output data for Shanghai in Tables 2 and 6.

Several conclusions can be drawn from these data taken together with additional qualitative evidence.

First, the peaks of activity were 1951, 1953 and 1956, while the accelerations which lead to these peaks began in mid-1950, autumn 1952 and spring 1956. Second, the private sector and the construction industry played important roles in these fluctuations – for not only did activity in these sectors usually fluctuate in the same direction as the aggregate data, but the intensity of fluctuation tended to be much greater.[1]

The peaks of activity and the relationship of them to sectoral fluctuations can be identified not only by statistical indicators, but also by abundant qualitative evidence of bottlenecks, and by the prevalence of certain types of economic behaviour which tended to be in evidence whenever economic activity was at high levels. Basically this latter may be described as behaviour prejudicial to the maintenance of control. We shall examine the implications of this in some detail shortly; the main point is that at the peaks, planners control over prices and resource use, particularly in the labour market and private sectors, was weakened, and that the desire to reassert control over the economy during the boom periods reinforced the importance of purely physical constraints on activity as a motive for dampening the level of activity. In practice this involved the reimposition of strict controls over the private and traditional

[1] The upturn in autumn 1950 followed the collapse of the urban economy in the spring of that year under the impact of draconian fiscal measures introduced to stabilise prices. See, Ch'ien Hua *et al.* chapter 2. Also, 'Shanghai's industry's stabilisation, recovery and development', *Ching chi chou pao* (The economic weekly, hereafter *CCCP*) Ser. 13, No. 23, 6 Dec. 1951, pp. 443–6. The upturn in 1952 followed a second economic crisis in the urban areas associated with the *wu fan* ('five antis') campaign which was a political movement directed against the power of the capitalist class. The 1956 upturn was related both to the stimulation of rural demand following the cooperativisation movement and the massive construction plan for 1956.

sector – almost irrespective of the effects of this on total output and employment.[1]

In the context of this study the most important characteristic of the peaks were periodic labour shortages which extended a long way down the skill and across the industry structure of the urban labour market. These shortages (which occurred in the context of growing structural unemployment) were directly responsible for loss of control over hiring and wages.

The significance of urban fluctuations for a whole range of economic management problems is so great that we must pause for a moment to consider why, during the 1950s, they were so severe. Several reasons stand out. First, there was the dependence of the urban economy on a fluctuating rural sector which supplied it with important inputs and was also a source of demand – particularly for the output of the small scale urban sector. Dependence of this type is common in developing countries but its importance was accentuated in China during the 1950s by a new degree and type of economic isolation from the outside world. For, whereas in the pre-war period imports could be obtained to counteract temporary shortfalls of the inputs normally supplied by domestic agriculture, and necessary for the functioning of the urban economy, after 1949 the imposition of stringent trade control and the commitment to a long term programme of capital goods imports precluded this form of stabilisation. Therefore in years when agricultural output and income were low the urban economy felt the full weight of readjustment implied by rural fluctuations.

A second explanation of the sharpness of fluctuations in the urban economy was the size of the private sector and its diminishing sensitivity to conventional economic controls. In considering the

[1] In late 1951 full capacity limits were being reported as reached in a wide variety of industrial sectors. See 'Vice Premier Ch'en Yün reports on economic and financial work', *CFJP* 26 Oct. 1951; 'In the last year commodity prices in our country have been basically stable', *CFJP* 24 Sep. 1951. In 1953, the pressure on the construction sector was the main destabilising factor and this led to an early and drastic revision of the annual plan. See, 'The East China Bureau of the Chinese Communist Party calls a meeting to discuss industrial production policy for the whole area', *CFJP* 14 Mar. 1953. For 1956 the best account is Po I-po, 'The out-turns of the 1956 national economic plan and the draft plan for 1957', *Hsin Hua pan yüeh k'an* (New China semi-monthly, hereafter *HHPYK*) 1957 No. 14, pp. 28–39.

size of the private sector we must remember that it included both capitalist enterprises in the modern sector and small scale production and trading activities of a traditional character. In terms of output it remained very important up to the end of 1953, and even up to 1957 it remained of some significance. In 1953, the private sector still accounted for 48·6% of total industrial and handicraft output and in some cities it was still preponderant. In Shanghai and Canton for example the private sector accounted for 63% and 65% of industrial output alone.[1] Furthermore it has to be appreciated that the private sector included the most labour intensive forms of activity in the urban sector (particularly in commerce) so that fluctuations in private sector output and sales lead to disproportionately large fluctuations in employment.

A basic explanation for the violence of private sector fluctuations was the increasing crudity of the instruments used for controlling it. Throughout the whole period the Government's attitude to capitalism and traditional forms of economic activity fluctuated sharply – being conditioned at any point in time by the degree to which these sectors were currently frustrating control of the economy and their importance in maintaining output and employment. The response – particularly of the capitalists – to these changing attitudes was correspondingly exaggerated. Thus when the Government was on the attack, the capitalists, foreseeing imminent extinction, closed their enterprises, and often, if the opportunity was open to them, migrated to Hong Kong. But when (as periodically happened) the capitalists became convinced of the Government's good intentions towards them, they reacted with the wild optimism of men entering a golden age. The problem was that as time passed and the reversals in Government policy multiplied, the sensitivity of the private sector to any stimulation or control seems to have declined. Thus, although between 1949 and 1952 the Government had some success in controlling the sector by conventional fiscal and monetary means, after the violent anti-capitalist campaign of the *wu fan* movement in mid-1952, the dominating consideration in the minds of the

[1] *1954 nien ch'üan kuo ke t'i shou kung yeh tiao ch'a tzu liao* (1954 national survey of individual handicraftsmen: materials), (1957). The handicraft output includes output in rural areas. Private industry's share of total industrial output in 1953 was 36·8%, *Ten great years*, p. 38.

capitalists was not whether marginal changes in budgetary, monetary or Government purchasing policy would make adjustment of their levels of activity worthwhile, but whether they were to be allowed to survive at all, and if so, for how long. This attitude meant that the Government had to resort to control techniques of increasing crudity and consequently of increasing potential for destabilisation.

A third factor in the severity of fluctuations was the adoption of a target rate of economic performance which was probably in excess of what was feasible in the long run, combined with a system of incentives and sanctions that induced a tendency to extremism in economic and indeed in all forms of activity. Hence, the economy alternated between booms in which plan targets were overshot at the expense of prodigal waste of resources and loss of control, and periods of relative stagnation during which the growth rate readjusted to its material base and the Party and planners struggled to reimpose control over economic institutions. These periods of stagnation were intensified by the effects of political repression with which they were invariably associated, and which seemed to be a necessary part of the process of reimposing control.

The exceptional character of the fluctuations in Shanghai can be explained in terms of the factors discussed above. The city had an abnormal dependence on agriculture because of the concentration in it of the cotton industry; it had an above average dependence on the private sector as is indicated in Tables 5 and 7; and finally, it was a city which, because of the extent of its historical association with foreigners, the size and excellence of its educational system and the size of its bureaucracy, was peculiarly vulnerable to purges and political movements of the type experienced in China in 1952, 1955 and 1957.

THE CHANGING INSTRUMENTS OF ECONOMIC CONTROL

The development of instruments of economic control in the cities was a gradual process. The cadres who found themselves responsible for the management of the urban economy in 1949 had been trained in an environment dominated by the logistics of guerrilla warfare and by the harvest – an environment in which almost all calculation was in real terms. In the cities, these cadres had to work in the context of political and economic relationships more complex and refined than any that they had previously encountered. In the longer run, the economic ambitions of the Government would require a whole new machinery of economic administration, but in 1949, although the apparatus of the Soviet State was an ideal which could be written about and admired, it was largely irrelevant to immediate problems. In the short run, the economy had to be managed by use of existing, conventional instruments, often operated with the assistance of existing non-communist personnel.

In the early years, the fiscal system was an important instrument of control. This system consisted of a hierarchy of geographical budgetary authorities (Province, Municipality, County, etc.), and of the budgetary system within each of the centrally controlled ministerial systems. The budgets of the geographical and ministerial authorities were combined to produce the overall, national budget.[1] In the period up to 1952, budgetary control was the main weapon used to control inflation, and its use required a tremendous drive to bring under control the budgets of the Great Administrative Areas and to discipline the activities of finance cadres throughout the whole system who had been accustomed to the freedoms of 'guerrilla style' finance work.[2]

During this period the principle was established that the obligations of each level of budgetary accounting to the level immediately superior were to take absolute precedence over all other claims on income. This principle, despite some modifications, was to have important repercussions until it was finally abandoned in 1958.[3]

In 1954 and 1955, the importance of budgetary work was again emphasised, although this time in the context of the acquisition of

[1] Good general accounts of the financial system are, Wang Ching-chih, *Wo kuo kuo chia yü suan* (Our country's national budget), (1956); Richard Diao, *Chung kung kuo min ching chi ts'ai cheng chi hua t'i hsi yü kung yeh ts'ai wu chi hua* (The economic and financial planning system in Communist China's national economy and industry), (1966).

[2] The 'guerilla style' of finance work was characterised by autonomy from central authorities; the use of local taxes (e.g. inter-county export/import charges); and tax policies and collection methods of a highly discriminatory and political character. See, 'Kwangtung finance progresses towards correct procedures', *Nan fang jih pao* (The southern daily, hereafter *NFJP*) 8 Sep. 1950.

[3] 'A discussion of the division of jurisdiction between central and local authorities in financial and economic work', *JMJP* 26 May 1951.

savings rather than of price control. The principle of the primacy of obligations to superior budgetary authorities was re-emphasised and reinforced by continuous auditing and in 1955, the share of the Central Government in total budgetary expenditure rose to a peak of 79%.[1]

There is abundant evidence that the effect of this growing professionalism and centralisation of the fiscal system prejudiced the maintenance of high levels of activity and the efficient use of resources. This was because the combination of rigidly enforced obligations and unpredictable tax revenues led to extreme conservatism in investment and other expenditure by local planning authorities. The impact of this on employment was particularly marked because local, labour intensive construction and small scale economic activities were affected by local budgetary squeezes. Similarly, financial conservatism *within* the ministerial systems also led to the immobilisation of investment resources.[2]

As a result of the experience of these years, the finance system underwent a process of decentralisation which started in 1956 and finished in 1958. An important outcome of this decentralisation, was that the budgetary authority of the municipal authorities was considerably enhanced.

Monetary policy was also of some importance in the period up to the end of 1952. The control of the banking system gave the authorities control over the supply and price of working capital and this was used to control the level of urban economic activity in a highly discriminatory manner. For example in 1950, it was used to mitigate some of the most serious effects of the draconian budgetary policy then being enforced to control inflation;[3] later – for example

[1] The planned share of Central Government in total expenditure in 1955 was 78·44%. In the 1954/55 budget speech the Finance Minister argued that an upward trend in the Central Government's share in spending was necessary and desirable if the Five Year Plans were to be financed successfully. See, Li Hsien-nien, 'Report on the out-turns of the 1954 budget and the estimates for 1955', *HHPYK* 1955 No. 8, pp. 23–32.

[2] A particularly interesting source of information on this subject is a series of budget accounts for Kwantung Province and Canton City between 1954 and 1956. The Provincial reports are in *NFJP* 17 Aug. 1954; *NFJP* 3 Dec. 1955; *NFJP* 5 Aug. 1956. The Canton City reports are in *Kwang chou jih pao* (Canton daily, hereafter *KCJP*) 7 Aug. 1954; *KCJP* 23 Nov. 1956. There is also a report for the small Kwangtung Municipality of Hai K'ou which throws very interesting light on the relationship between a Provincial and a minor budgetary authority, see, *NFJP* 16 Aug. 1956.

[3] See, 'The volume of loans expands every month', *CFJP* 12 May 1950; 'In all areas the phenomenon of closures is steadily disappearing', *Shang hai kung shang tzu liao*

after the *wu fan* in 1952 – it was again used in a highly selective fashion as an instrument to make the Government's control of the private sector more effective.[1] After this period, however, the sensitivity of the private sector to monetary policy declined markedly so that other techniques of control had to be developed.

The main source of new power over the economy in our period was the expansion of the public sector and the formal planning apparatus. This expansion is illustrated in Table 5 and in Table 10 above which show the declining share of the private sector in industrial output and retail commerce. Of course control was not simply a function of the size of the state sector, for within that sector the planners had to develop information systems and a structure of incentives and sanctions which ensured the responsiveness of the economic administrators at the enterprise level. This quest for control was never wholly successful and led to experiments in organisation in which the Party and Mass Organisations played important roles. Nonetheless, despite the existence of problems within the public sector, the socialisation of 1956 marked in principle the point at which the authorities assumed complete control over all urban economic decisions, and it is significant that the national economic plan for 1957 was probably the most intelligent and technically satisfactory annual economic plan for the whole period.

Finally, it is important for our purposes to note that the changes in economic administration which were necessitated by the socialisation and the decentralisation of the finance and economic systems, initiated a chain of events which transformed the importance of the municipality as an economic planning unit. Before 1956, the municipality governments had of course performed a wide range of functions. For apart from a whole array of non-economic work, departments of the municipal governments played an important role in the allocation of industrial materials, food and labour and had been responsible for the operation of state enterprises not under

(Materials on private industry and commerce in Shanghai), 19 Jul. 1950. In this early period there were some quite sophisticated discussions about interest rate policy. For example, 'Some views on lowering interest rates', *CCCP* Ser. 10, No. 24, 15 Jun. 1950, pp. 9–10.

[1] 'Discuss the present stage of bank work', *CCCP* No. 26, 3 Sep. 1952, pp. 507–9.

direct ministerial control. In 1956, the municipal authorities also assumed responsibility for everything previously in the private sector, and in 1957, for those enterprises shed by the central ministries in the decentralisation of that year. This acquisition of responsibility for production and trading enterprises had to be accompanied by new powers to plan and coordinate the supply of raw materials and labour. Thus by the late 1950s, the municipality had become a planning unit of major importance, and had powers and responsibilities greater probably than those of comparable authorities in the cities of any other country in the world.

THE UNRESOLVED PROBLEMS OF URBAN ECONOMIC MANAGEMENT

The basic problem that the managers of the urban economy were unable to solve in the period 1949 to 1957, was that of reconciling the objectives of maintaining very high levels of urban economic activity and employment and at the same time maintaining control over prices and resource use, notably in the labour market.

Let us consider first the period up to 1956. In this period, high levels of output and employment required a high level of activity in the private sector. This was recognised in 1950, in the context of unemployment and a 'scissors crisis';[1] and in 1952 in the context of a renewed employment crisis and of the control figures for the first year of the Five Year Plan.[2] Yet the events of 1951 and 1953 showed that, when stimulated, the private sector rapidly went out of control and developed a capacity to frustrate the planned growth of the public sector. The reason for this was that as the level of activity rose, so did the financial strength of the private sector and its power to bid up the prices of raw materials and labour; to negotiate higher prices for Government contracts; and even to refuse such contracts

[1] See particularly, 'Overall arrangements and concern for both sides is the only way', *JMJP* 4 Jun. 1950; 'Financial and economic work in the Chinese People's Republic during the past year', *JMJP* 1 Oct. 1950.
[2] 'State concerns in Shanghai help private firms to expand', *New China News Agency* (hereafter *NCNA*) release, translated in *Survey of the China mainland press* 395 (hereafter *SCMP*), 13 Aug. 1952.

should such a course seem profitable.[1]

Attempts were made to exercise detailed control over private firms through the activities of Union officials, Party members and other political activists within these firms, as well as through the working of the monetary and fiscal system, but these efforts were never successful in the long run because the authorities had neither the administrative nor political resources necessary to control the large number of small enterprises involved.[2]

Thus, given that the periodic growth of the private economic sector, which stimulation of the urban economy involved, was unacceptable; and given the failure of conventional economic or internal political controls, the outcome of these expansions were campaigns of direct political and legal intimidation which succeeded at the price of a general lowering of the level of economic activity and employment.[3] When the latter had fallen to intolerable levels, the authorities had to initiate another round of stimulation which led to further loss of control. Our conclusion is, therefore, that the survival of a substantial private sector until 1956 made the policy objectives

[1] The volume and terms of state contracts become the most important of the conventional techniques for controlling the private sector after the *wu fan* (five antis) campaign. For details of resistance in 1951 see, Wu Chiang, *Chung kuo tzu pen chu i kai tsao wen t'i* (Problems in the economic reform of Chinese capitalism), (1958), chapter 3; 'A refutation of "free development" thought arising out of the improvement in industry and trade', *HWJP* 24 Sep. 1951. For 1953, see, 'Private industrial and commercial circles in Shenyang begin a movement to implement the correct style of work in management', *Ta kung pao* (The impartial daily, hereafter *TKP*), (Tientsin) 17 Oct. 1953. Data on profit trends in the private sector are in 'The reform of Shanghai's private industry and commerce during the past four years', *JMJP* 3 Mar. 1954.

[2] The main form of non-economic control over the private sector in the early 1950s were quasi-democratic bodies consisting of representatives of management, unions, the Party and workers. These were introduced very early on and strengthened somewhat in 1952. These initiatives do not seem to have met with much success and in 1954 a final effort was made to establish control of the private sector through groups of political activists within enterprises. In Shanghai, a special training school was established to prepare workers for the 'bitter and complex' struggle ahead. See, *Kung ch'ang kuan li min chu hua* (The democratisation of factory management), (1950); 'Output and quality generally up; relations between labour and capital improved', *CFJP* 8 Jan. 1953; 'Train the Party backbone in private enterprise', *CFJP* 15 Feb. 1954.

[3] In 1954, for example, the private sector was subject to a widely publicised stream of legal actions against capitalists who were held to have contravened tax, labour and other laws. See, 'Ch'iu Kao-hsi the capitalist proprietor of the Te Hsing factory in Shanghai is given a prison sentence', *TKP* (Peking) 17 Apr. 1954 and 'The Canton Municipality People's Court convenes a public sentencing assembly and passes sentence on the illegal actions of a batch of capitalists', *NFJP* 12 Jul. 1954. Legal intimidation was also used again in 1957, see, 'Stop capitalist counter currents', *TKP* (Peking) 16 Aug. 1957.

of maintaining effective economic control and high levels of urban activity mutually incompatible, and that this incompatibility generated a policy cycle that was an important component of the total pattern of urban economic fluctuations. Moreover, as argued earlier, this cycle was explosive since the increasing insensitivity of the private sector necessitated the use of controls whose violence carried ever greater potential for destabilisation.

The special problems of the private sector were not however the only explanation of the inability of the planners to reconcile control with high levels of activity in this period. The behaviour of administrators in the public sector was also important – particularly in the periodic destabilisation of the labour market. This was notably the case in 1953 and 1956 when the planned construction expansion and the pressure for fulfilment of very high physical output targets resulted in a partial collapse of hiring and wage controls. We shall explore this further in later chapters.

The socialisation of the private sector in 1956 was expected to resolve many of these problems. For the socialisation ensured that, formally, all economic decisions could be made by the planners; and in theory this implied that they could put as much pressure on the urban economy as they wished without risking loss of control; thus making possible the fulfilment of the very ambitious construction and output plans for 1956 without recrudescence of the control problems of 1951 and 1953. However in practice the matter was more complex; for the acquisition of formal powers over economic enterprises could only be meaningful in so far as administrative and political control over them was really effective. Unfortunately it was not. In Shanghai, for example, we find the municipal planners admitting in August 1956 that they were still only capable of planning *directly* 23% of the output for which they had been responsible since the January socialisation; and in practice, the operation of all enterprises previously in the private sector depended largely on the goodwill and cooperation of the old capitalists, managers and intellectuals.[1] It was precisely the necessity of securing this goodwill that lead the Government to combine the 'High Tide of Socialism'

[1] See especially K'o Ch'ing-shih, secretary of the Shanghai Bureau of the Central Committee of the Communist Party in *CFJP* 11 Aug. 1956. The weakness of political

in the cities with an era of political liberalisation and subsequently a wage reform that favoured possessors of technical and managerial skills. It was no accident that Chou En-lai's famous liberalising speech on 'The Problem of Intellectuals' was made on the eve of the last, extraordinary week of the Shanghai socialisation.[1]

The defects of socialisation as a strategy for control rapidly revealed themselves, and in the autumn of 1956 and in 1957 we find yet another revival of the 'private sector'. This now consisted of handicraft cooperatives and small enterprises which were in the public sector, yet in practice capable of independent action, and also the so-called 'autonomous enterprises'. The former were mainly enterprises and handicraft shops which had been in the private sector before January 1956 but which had not been effectively incorporated into the planning system; they exhibited strong tendencies to independent action which the authorities described as 'commercialism' and 'capitalism'.[2]

The 'autonomous enterprises' were illegal firms, staffed by peasants, unemployed workers, housewives, ex-members of disintegrating cooperatives and others anxious to participate in the urban work force, but unable to do so in the public sector (or in some cases only able to do so at unsatisfactory levels of income).[3] Most of the autonomous enterprises were initially very small, but they showed a surprising propensity to grow both in terms of turnover and geographical linkages. Thus the dilemma of 1951 and

---

control is indicated in Shanghai by the fact that there were only 49,982 Party members in Shanghai in 1956, in which year it was reported that there were over 26,000 enterprises in the industrial sector alone. It seems certain, therefore, that there must have been large numbers of economic enterprises in which there was not even a single Party member. See, *HWJP* 8 Aug. 1956; *CFJP* 27 Jul. 1956.

[1] The Shanghai socialisation was completed in the third week in January (although only a few weeks earlier it had been expected that the socialisation process would take another ten years). Chou En-lai's speech was made on 14 January. See, *Cheng chih hsüeh hsi* (Political study) No. 2, 13 Feb. 1956; *Lao tung pao* (Labour daily, hereafter *LTP*) 20 Nov. 1955; *LTP* 25 Nov. 1955; *JMJP* 19–22 Jan. 1956.

[2] In the public sector in Shanghai in 1957 there were estimated to be at least 20,000 enterprises whose production was not subject to direct planning – indeed a great many of these enterprises could *not* be planned, because they did not at that time keep any accounts. See, *CFJP* 11 Aug. 1956.

[3] The number of autonomous enterprises in Shanghai in March 1957 was given as 5,000. These enterprises were classified under ninety different industries and trades and employed a total of 16,000 workers. 'Strengthen the management of autonomous enterprises', *CFJP* 3 Mar. 1957.

1953 presented itself yet again. For the new private sector proved to be as unmanageable as the old. It frustrated control over materials supply and prices and it undermined employment and wage control in the public sector. Yet the sector was tolerated (at least in part) until the Great Leap Forward, and nowhere in the 1950s is the conflict between the desire to maintain high levels of output and employment and the unwillingness to acquiesce in the loss of control that this entailed, more apparent than in the handling of the autonomous enterprises in 1957. Firm measures were taken against 'capitalist tendencies' within the public sector; but although the autonomous enterprises were threatened again and again, they were always reprieved from complete extinction on the grounds that the employment and output they provided made them indispensible.[1]

Apart from this, the problem of controlling the large enterprises in the public sector when under pressure had not been solved by 1957 either. For in 1956 we find that the materials supply and employment and wage work were as chaotic as ever. To some extent this can be attributed to the inevitable confusion of a transition period: but in the longer run, events suggest that only a decentralisation more radical than anything contemplated in 1956, combined with a greater degree of Party control than anything experienced in the early 1950s, would give the Government the power it wanted.

To summarise, the main features of the urban economy in the 1950s were rapid population growth; rapid but erratic growth of industrial output; and a transformation of economic institutions and instruments of control which, although radical, did not enable the planners to reconcile the objectives of high levels of urban economic activity and employment *and* the maintenance of controls sufficient to ensure the consistent fulfilment of plan targets.

---

[1] 'Supervision by the masses must be strengthened', *CFJP* 22 Mar. 1957; 'Heads of small firms in Shanghai attend the first lesson [in the correct style of management]', *CFJP* 20 Oct. 1957. In defence of the private sector see, 'Why tolerate autonomous enterprises?', *HWJP* 11 May 1957 and speeches at the National Handicrafts Conference in December 1957, *TKP* (Peking) 24 Dec. 1957.

2

THE GROWTH AND STRUCTURE OF THE URBAN LABOUR FORCE

In this chapter we have to consider the problems of quantifying China's urban employment experience. Comprehensive official data on this subject are slight and up to the present there have been only two completely original attempts to provide the sort of statistical framework relevant to our needs. Neither of these is wholly satisfying.

The most detailed and comprehensive manpower estimates at present available are those of J. P. Emerson.[1] Wherever possible we have made use of Emerson's estimates in this book but the data have limitations which justify the attempt to find alternative approaches to the problem of measuring China's urban employment trends. The main problem with these data is that they are concerned with the whole of the non-agricultural labour force. They therefore include persons resident in rural areas and engaged in occupations such as construction, trade, services and education. Since such persons have been estimated to form *a majority* of all non-agricultural employment, changes in this category of employment can only be of restricted interest to those concerned with economic change and labour markets in urban areas.[2]

The second difficulty with Emerson's data is the inaccuracy which arises from the fact that they are basically a reconstruction of official data which are themselves defective due to systematic under-reporting. This under-reporting was partly due to the slow development of a centralised and effective statistical system; this factor precluded the collection of comprehensive and consistently defined employment data, particularly in the early 1950s. Information on the

---

[1] Emerson (1965).

[2] Liu Ta-chung and Yeh Kung-chia, *The Economy of the Chinese Mainland: national income and economic development, 1933–1959* (1965), pp. 102–3. Liu and Yeh estimate that the rural component of the non-agricultural labour force was 67%.

public sector was fairly adequate and there was considerable information on persons classified as workers and staff.[1] Outside these categories, however, comprehensive time series did not exist. A second source of under-reporting in the official data is the deliberate exclusion and under-counting of persons engaged in traditional trades and services, capitalists and persons engaged in various other kinds of illicit activities which were not considered worthy enough to be counted as employment in a socialist society.

These sources of under-reporting declined in the 1950s and Emerson has been able to make some allowance for this in his estimates. However, as he himself makes clear, his figures probably still reflect the biases of the official data.

The second set of estimates of interest is that made by T. C. Liu and K. C. Yeh as part of their comprehensive work on economic growth in China between 1933 and 1962.[2] Comparison of Liu and Yeh's results with those of Emerson provides striking evidence of the scope for disagreement which national employment estimates provide. For example Emerson's estimate of non-agricultural employment in 1957 (allowing for under-counting) is 44,000,000; which compares with Liu and Yeh's estimate of 64,000,000. This difference is partly based on a different handling of the problem of persons living in rural areas and engaged in both the agricultural and non-agricultural sector. But the fact that discrepancies of this order of magnitude are possible demonstrates to us how great the difficulties in making national manpower estimates are and how elusive the concept of non-agricultural employment really is.

Another area in which the measurement of employment change is particularly difficult is that of unemployment. Scattered official data were published on urban unemployment in the early 1950s and again in 1956 and 1957. These data put urban unemployment at

[1] The category of 'workers and staff' includes all persons who are basically wage earners. It therefore excludes capitalists, petty traders and handicraftsmen, temporary construction workers and others whose income is variable. 'The problems of defining the numbers of our workers and staff at the present time', *T'ung chi kung tso* (Statistical work, hereafter *TCKT*) 1957 No. 1, pp. 19–20. In Shanghai in 1956 approximately 70% of those in employment were workers and staff. 'The livelihood of the city's workers and staff has markedly improved', *HWJP* 2 Sep. 1957 and Table 17.

[2] Liu and Yeh.

about 3,000,000 in 1950 and 1,000,000 in 1956.[1] These figures however were usually based either on unemployment registers which systematically under-stated the problem, or on crude sample surveys which excluded unemployed workers from the traditional sectors and women who wished to enter the labour force.

Emerson has attempted to estimate the growth of unemployment in urban areas by juxtaposing official data on migration and the increase of the indigenous population of working age, with his own estimates of the growth of workers and staff in urban areas. This yields an increase of urban unemployment of 2,000,000 during the First Five Year Plan.[2] This cannot be considered satisfactory, however, since it relies on the accuracy of official aggregate data in an area where there is good reason for doubt, and since also it equates the urban work force with the numbers of workers and staff, when we know that the former was substantially larger than the latter and that the changes in the one were by no means always in the same direction as changes in the other.

Liu and Yeh's approach to the problem is to compare estimates of the urban population of working age with their estimates of urban employment.[3] The fundamental defect of this approach is that it cannot handle the problem of women who are not participating in the labour force but who wish that they were. Since there is no way of distinguishing this type of involuntary unemployment from voluntary abstention from the workforce, Liu and Yeh have to restrict their estimates of unemployment to the male sex. This must do some violence to reality, since as we shall see later, there were strong normative and economic pressures on women to participate in economic work, which given the slow growth of employment must imply considerable involuntary unemployment in the 1950s.

Liu and Yeh's results are more pessimistic about unemployment than Emerson's in that for the First Plan period they estimate that male unemployment alone increased by 4,000,000 – double Emerson's estimate for total unemployment.

[1] 'The road to employment is a broad one', *JMJP* 19 Jan. 1957; Liao Lu-yen, 'An explanation of the National Plan for Agricultural Development 1956–1967', in *1956 nien tao 1967 nien ch'üan kuo nung yeh fa chan kang yao (ts'ao an)* (The draft National Plan for Agricultural Development, 1956–67), (1956).
[2] Emerson in *The Profile*, Vol. 2, p. 419.　　[3] Liu and Yeh, pp. 102–3.

Examination of the methods of these important scholars shows how the two basic alternative approaches to the problem both involve difficulties which at present seem almost insuperable. Emerson on the one hand, departs as rarely as possible from the official figures and as a result cannot escape from the defects in such data. Liu and Yeh, on the other hand, start with a small collection of pre- and post-1949 data which they can only convert into a detailed set of estimates by making assumptions that are frequently incapable of justification.[1] Thus Emerson's results are incomplete but have the merit of giving us some important information, while Liu and Yeh give results in a form which is useful and consistent, but whose final value is affected by reservations about their accuracy and the omission of the female unemployed.

In view of the difficulties of assembling national employment data that are both credible and analytically useful, it seemed worthwhile attempting to construct a picture of urban employment change based on data for individual cities. This approach eliminates some of the difficulties encountered in estimating and handling highly aggregated data, and by restricting oneself to individual cities one can use employment data in direct conjunction with demographic and production data, and, with the aid of systematic qualitative information of the kind available for many cities, one can build up a coherent if at times incomplete description of the working of individual urban economies.

The population, migration and employment data available for some cities are more detailed and probably more accurate than national data on these subjects, and it must be the case that such data are superior to those which include (or are derived from) the experience of rural areas.

In this book we have concentrated on the experience of Shanghai but have tried to supplement this with data on other cities where possible. This supplementation does not attempt to be a fully controlled comparative analysis but is concerned rather to illustrate some of the diversity of China's economic experience and to show the scope that exists for further work of a comparative nature.

[1] The assumption, for example, that the *rate* of unemployment is the same in urban and rural areas.

POPULATION, MIGRATION, AND EMPLOYMENT IN
SHANGHAI

In this section we shall first present some data on the growth of Shanghai's population and then proceed to estimate the supply and demand for non-agricultural labour between 1949 and 1957; the net change in non-agricultural employment in that period; and finally, the structure of employment in 1957 and evidence of long-run trends in this.

Total population is estimated to have grown from 5 millions to 7·2 millions between late 1949 and the end of 1957. This represents a growth rate of 4·7% per annum. In Table 11 below some official data for the intervening years are also included but we have made no effort to interpolate the missing years.

Of the total population increase we estimate that 33·6% was due to net migration and the remaining 66·4% to natural increase.[1]

The supply of labour

The supply of job seekers in the Shanghai population came from three sources: the natural addition to the labour force; the migrant addition to the labour force; and the stock of unemployed persons – which included both persons unemployed in 1949 and persons who subsequently lost employment.

In order to estimate the natural addition to the labour force it is necessary to define the labour force in terms of age and make some assumption about the age structure of the population at the beginning of the period. We have defined the age limits of the working population as sixteen to sixty and we have estimated the age structure of the population in 1949 by using detailed age structure data for 1930, adjusted in the light of a small but important piece of information about the age structure in 1947.[2]

Applying our estimate of the age structure to the 1949 population

[1] From data in Table 12 and, 'Reduce the natural rate of population growth in Shanghai to 2%', *WHP* 23 Jan. 1958.

[2] Pre-war data from *Statistics of Shanghai compiled in 1933* (1933), table IV, p. 3. The data for 1947 is in Wang Shan-pao, 'Research into Shanghai city's grain consumption', *She hui yüeh k'an* (Monthly journal of the Bureau of Social Affairs, Shanghai, hereafter *SHYK*), Ser. 3, No. 5, 5 May 1948, p. 36.

Table 11. *The population of Shanghai, 1949–65 (urban and rural)*

	millions									
	1949	1950	1951	1952	1953	1954	1955	1956	1957	1965
Total	5·0[a]	5·4[b]	–	–	6·2[d]	–	6·5[e]	6·75[f]	7·2[h]	10·0[i]
of which										
Rural	–	·245[c]	–	–	–	–	–	·400[g]	–	4·0[j]

SOURCES:

[a] This is our estimate. 'We must make a great effort to persuade peasants who have migrated into the city to return to the countryside voluntarily', *CFJP* 31 Jul. 1955.

[b, c] These figures are given in *Tu pao shou ts'e* (The newspaper reader's handbook), (1950).

[d] This is the 1953 Census figure quoted in Morris B. Ullman, *Cities of mainland China: 1953–1958* (1961), p. 22.

[e] In April 1955 the population reached a peak of 7,000,000, 'Why we must reduce Shanghai's population', *HWJP* 10 Aug. 1955. The reduction in population in the early summer of that year is estimated to have brought the total down to 6,500,000 by the end of the year.

[f] A figure of 6,570,000 was given as the year-end population by Chang Jui, 'Some views on Shanghai's population and area', *WHP* 11 Feb. 1957. This however explicitly excluded persons in the process of being removed from the city who were in fact still resident there. A more realistic indication of population at this time is probably the figure for January 1957 of 6,800,000. This is given in 'Mobilise peasants to return to rural production', *CFJP* 10 Mar. 1957.

[g] Chang Jui, work cited in note *f*.

[h] Population continued to rise under the impact of immigration at least until September 1957 when a total of 7,250,000 was reported. See, 'Shanghai's population reaches 7,250,000', *WHP* 17 Nov. 1957. Forced emigration then began to take effect and for the year-end total we have used a figure given for January 1958, in *WHP* 6 Jun. 1958.

[i, j] During 1958 the total area under the administration of the Shanghai Government was enlarged by ten counties so that population data after that year are no longer comparable with earlier figures. The data for 1965 are those given to visitors and are the same as those in the *Economic Geography of East China* published in 1959. Sun Ching-chih and others, *Hua Tung ti ch'ü ching chi ti li* (An economic geography of East China), (1959), p. 44.

produces an estimate of the natural addition to the labour force of 697,000. To obtain the actual flow of job seekers this figure has to be adjusted to allow for the effect of retentions within the educational system of persons within the relevant age group. The effect of such retentions will depend on whether or not there was a *net* inflow or outflow from the educational system of persons aged sixteen or over. This in turn will depend on whether the student population of the relevant age group was increasing or not; for if the system was of constant size, after the first group of students had graduated the inflow of new enrolments would be exactly offset by the outflow of graduates. There is no doubt that there was in fact a rapid increase in the educational retention between 1949 and 1957 and we have estimated that the net off-take from the labour market amounted to 144,000 persons. The net flow of job seekers from the indigenous population is therefore estimated to 553,000.[1]

It will be noted that this estimate of the natural increase of the labour force assumes that *all* young women wish to work. This may not have been strictly the case but any young women who did not wish to work would almost certainly have been at least offset by women over sixteen in 1949 who were not then in employment, but subsequently wished to be so. This is an imperfect solution to the problem of involuntary female unemployment but seems preferable to approaches that have to fall back on estimates of male labour supply only.

We now have to consider the size of the migrant addition to the labour force. In Table 12 below we present a summary of population movements into and out of Shanghai for 1949 to 1957.

Table 12. *A summary of population movements into and out of Shanghai, 1949–57*

	(000's)	
	Immigration	Emigration
	1,000[a] (to 1955)	
	820[b] (1956/57)	
	Total 1,820	Total 1,080[c]
	Net immigration	
	Total 740	**1607332**

SOURCES:
[a] 'We must persuade peasants who have infiltrated into the city to return voluntarily to the countryside', *CFJP* 31 Jul. 1955.
[b, c] Hsü Chien-kuo (Vice-Mayor of Shanghai), 'Mobilise surplus urban labour power to help construct socialist agriculture', *WHP* 7 Jan. 1958.

[1] Strictly, the relevant parts of the educational system are the Upper Middle Schools (16–18 years) and the higher educational system. However there is evidence of over-age students in the Lower Middle Schools and allowance has to be made for this. Our

In order to draw any conclusions about the effect of these migrations on the labour force we need to know something about the types of people involved. Let us consider immigration first. Reported immigration amounted to 1,820,000 persons of whom 1,000,000 migrated before April 1955 and the rest in 1956–57. We have evidence that suggests that half of these persons were job seekers.[1] The gross addition to the labour force through immigration is therefore put at 910,000.

The question of emigration is more complicated. Emigration for the whole period was reported as being 1,080,000 and this number was broken down in one official source into the following four categories.

Table 13. *Categories of emigrants from Shanghai, 1949–57*

	(000's)
1. Persons assigned to employment in other cities	260
2. Persons (and their families) returned to work in rural areas	780
3. Persons sent to open new land	30
4. Unspecified balance	10
Total	1, 080

SOURCE: Hsü Chien-kuo, *WHP* 7 Jan. 1958.

The total number of emigrants shown in this table may be compared with the total shown in Table 14 which shows the reported

estimate of the Shanghai off-take was arrived at in the following way. First, we assembled data of enrolments and graduations for *all* Junior and Senior Middle Schools and institutions of higher education. These data were adjusted for drop-outs and for an estimate that one third of Junior Middle School pupils were of working age. An estimate of the net inflow into the national educational system was then made. Shanghai's share in this was assumed to be proportional to its share of the total student population. Finally, the Shanghai off-take was adjusted to allow for the assumption that 40% of the student population came from rural areas. National data in *Ten great years*, p. 192, 'Problems of the development plan for our country's Junior and Middle Schools', *Chi hua ching chi* (Planned economy, hereafter *CHCC*) No. 10, 9 Oct. 1957, pp. 20–7, and 'The development of our country's educational activity in recent years', *TCKT* No. 20, 29 Oct. 1956, pp. 5–6. We have included in our calculations an allowance for the 78,000 people in Shanghai who in 1957 were being educated completely outside the formal educational system. Shanghai data in *WHP* 9 Aug. 1956; *HWJP* 15 Aug. 1956; *WHP* 13 Apr. 1957; *WHP* 16 Apr. 1957; *WHP* 17 Apr. 1957.
    [1] Hsü Chien-kuo, work cited in Table 12. This article gives a fairly detailed breakdown of the characteristics of immigrants to Shanghai in 1956.

annual emigration flows. The slight discrepancy between the two is probably accounted for by the return of refugees in 1950 which was not reported at the time.

Table 14. *Emigration from Shanghai, 1949–57*

					(000's)					
Category	1949	1950	1951	1952	1953	1954	1955	1956	1957	Total
1	–	16[a]	–	–	24[b]	30[c]	59[d]	123[f]	6[g]	258
1[a]	–	16[a]	–	–	24[b]	–	23[e]	–	6[g]	(69)
2	50[h]	–	–	–	–	–	560[i]	–	140[j]	750
3	–	–	–	–	40[k]	–	–	–	–	40
4	10[l]	–	–	–	–	–	–	–	–	10

Total 1,058

Category 1 Persons assigned to employment in other cities.
Category 1a Persons assigned as category 1 but described as skilled workers and staff or cadres.
Category 2 Persons returned to work in rural areas and their families.
Category 3 Persons sent to open new land.
Category 4 Persons sent to labour reform.

SOURCES: data in or derived from,
[a, b] 'Shanghai industry helps national construction', *WHP* 27 Aug. 1954. 'A large batch of skilled workers in the city give in their names to participate in national key-point construction', *WHP* 22 Jun. 1954.
[c] '220,000 workers sent from Shanghai to take part in construction in various places', *NCNA* (Shanghai) 16 Sep. 1957. Sung Li-wen 'Report on the implementation of the Shanghai National Economic Plan in 1956 and on the Plan for 1967', *HWJP* 28 Aug. 1957.
[d] Sung Li-wen, work cited in note *c*.
[e] To March 1956. 'The Shanghai Municipality Communist Party decides that in future Shanghai industry will be fully and rationally developed', *CFJP* 27 Jul. 1956.
[f] Work cited in note *c*. *NCNA* (Shanghai) 16 Sep. 1957.
[g] These were all cadres. See 'A new high tide of cadres being sent down [to the countryside] from Shanghai', *WHP* 3 Jan. 1958.
[h] 'Almost 50,000 refugees have been organised and returned [to their homes in the countryside]', *CFJP* 21 Aug. 1949.
[i] Chang Jui, 'Some views on Shanghai's population and area', *WHP* 11 Feb. 1957.
[j] 'Almost 140,000 returned to rural production', *HWJP* 20 Dec. 1957.
[k] 'The Kansu consolation organisation holds a consolation conference', *CFJP* 13 Feb. 1957.
[l] 'More than 10,000 men just off to open waste land', *CFJP* 7 Mar. 1950.

We can now estimate the effect of migration on the labour force. It is assumed that categories 1, 3 and 4 were all members of the labour force, and since those in category 2 were nearly all peasants, we assume that 50% of them were members of the labour force. Thus the total loss to the labour force due to emigration was 690,000. This may be deducted from the immigrant addition to the labour force to leave a net gain of 220,000.

We now have estimates for the addition to the labour force due to natural growth and migration. To obtain the total number of job seekers we must add the number estimated to have been unemployed in 1949 to the number who lost employment between that year and the end of 1957.[1] This gives a combined total of 671,000. From this however, we must deduct something for the number of the un-employed who would have reached sixty by 1957 and who may therefore be considered as having retired. Using pre-war age data this is estimated at 134,000.

The demand for labour

We now require a figure for the total supply of jobs between 1949 and 1957. The official figure for the number of job openings in Shanghai up to the end of 1956 is 530,000,[2] and we can make an adjustment to this to allow for additional employment which was generated in various ways in 1957. This gives us a final total of 640,000.[3]

We can now incorporate all the above data in a balance sheet showing the demand and supply for labour. This is done in Table 15 below. It will be seen that we are left with a balance of 670,000 unemployed in 1957.

In view of the uncertainty that surrounds the labour supply data in this table, the figure for employment can only be regarded as a crude estimate of the order of magnitude of open unemployment in

[1] 'The number in employment rises by 630,000', *CFJP* 16 Aug. 1957; *Ch'ang chiang jih pao* (The Yangtze River daily, hereafter *CCJP*) 20 Jan. 1950.

[2] The figure of 530,000 is in 'One person in three has employment', *JMJP* 19 Aug. 1957. The additional 110,000 for 1957 is an estimate based on data in the following, 'The Shanghai Labour Bureau's method of settling the unemployed is a good one', *JMJP* 7 Oct. 1957; 'Shanghai thoroughly cleans up and reorganises autonomous enterprises', *TKP* 19 Aug. 1957 (Peking); 'The city's small traders must continue to advance along the socialist road', *HWJP* 18 Jan. 1957; 'Concerning the reform of private commerce and supply work', *CFJP* 17 Jan. 1956; 'The number of peripatetic pedlars is ever increasing', *HWJP* 27 May 1957.

[3] This total of 530,000 compares with a total of 519,000 obtained by summing the reported data of annual gross additions to employment quoted in Table 31 in Chapter 4.

Table 15. *The supply of job seekers and the supply of non-agricultural employment in Shanghai, 1949–57*

Job seekers		(000's)
the natural addition to the labour force (net of the educational retention)	553	(42%)
the net migrant addition to the labour force	220	(17%)
unemployment carried over from pre-1949 and subsequently generated	537	(41)%
Total	1,310	(100%)
The supply of employment	640	
Unemployment	670	

Shanghai in the late 1950s. Unfortunately we have no data which enable us to estimate variations in hours worked or the impact of seasonal factors – which must have been important in the cotton and construction industries and in the traditional sector in general. If such data were available, sophisticated measures of labour utilisation would make the situation look even more serious than that indicated by our estimate of open unemployment.

The only check that we have been able to make on our estimate has been to use the age and sex structure data for the population in conjunction with data on total and female employment in 1957, to make an estimate of *male* unemployment in that year. We have done this and the conclusion is that total male unemployment in 1957 was 560,000; this seems consistent with our total figure for unemployment.[1]

The net change in non-agricultural employment, 1949–57

We are in a position to estimate the net change in non-agricultural employment between 1949 and 1957. This can be done by deducting an estimate of the *net* increase in non-agricultural employment from the estimate of total non-agricultural employment for 1957. Total employment in that year is put at 2,418,000 and since net additional employment is estimated to have been 233,000 between 1949 and 1957, we reach a figure of 2,185,000 for total employment in 1949.[2]

[1] For a full account of this see, Christopher Howe, 'The level and structure of employment and the sources of labour supply in Shanghai', in John Wilson Lewis, *The city in Communist China* (1971).
[2] The 1957 level of employment is estimated from *NCNA* release, 17 Jan. 1957 and

The structure of employment in Shanghai

In Tables 16–19 below we present data on the structure of employment in Shanghai in 1957 and contrast these with data for earlier years. The detailed estimate of employment structure in 1957 involves some hazardous assumptions but the main features of the table are not in doubt. The conclusions to be drawn from these tables are discussed in our general conclusions on the growth and change in the Shanghai labour force below.

Table 16. *The structure of employment in Shanghai in 1957*

	(000's)
Industry, total	899
of which: modern factory	(770)
workshop	(129)
Handicrafts, total	258
of which: peripatetic and household	(38)
workshops employing less than ten men	(71)
individual handicraftsmen and others	(149)
Other small scale production	30
Construction	30
Transport, total	177
of which: the modern, public system	(57)
pedicabs	(40)
carts	(80)
Stevedores	33
Commerce, total	533
of which: old private sector stores	(221)
pedlars	(240)
old public sector commerce system	(72)
Food and services	50
Education	72
Health	30
Banking	25
Government, Mass Organisations and other (residual)	281
Total	2,418

SOURCES: See Appendix.

The development of the Shanghai labour force: conclusions

These materials give us a fairly clear picture of employment changes

data cited on p. 38. The net increase in employment after 1949 is calculated by deducting from the gross increase allowances for retirement, deaths, disabsorptions, and the transfer to other cities of persons in employment in Shanghai. The figure arrived at is closely confirmed by the article of Wang Shan-pao cited on p. 33.

Table 17. *The structure of employment in Shanghai by main sectors in 1957*

Sector	Total (000's)	%
Agriculture[a]	160	6·2
Factory production	770	29·9
Traditional production	417	16·2
Transport and communications[b]	210	8·1
Construction	30	1·2
Commerce	533	20·7
Food and services	50	1·9
Government, education, health, banking	408	15·8
	2,578	100·0

SOURCES:
[a] This assumes that 40% of the rural population were wholly engaged in agricultural work, see Christopher Howe, 'The level and structure of employment and the sources of labour supply in Shanghai', in Lewis.
[b] Includes stevedores.
Other data as Table 16.

Table 18. *The structure of non-agricultural employment in Shanghai by traditional and modern sectors in 1957*

Modern sector	Totals (000's)	%	Traditional sector	Totals (000's)	%
Industry	770	56·2	Workshop industry	129	12·3
Construction	30	2·2	Handicrafts[b]	288	27·5
Transport and communication[a]	90	6·5	Transport	120	11·4
Commerce	72	5·3	Commerce[c]	461	44·0
Education, health, banking and other	408	29·8	Food and services	50	4·8
Total	1,370	100·0	Total	1,048	100·0

SOURCES: As Table 17.
[a] Includes stevedores.
[b] Includes 'other small scale production'.
[c] Includes a few persons engaged in stores which should be classified as modern.

Table 19. *The structure of employment in Shanghai by main sectors:*
1926/27 and 1957

Sector	(%)	
	1926/27[a]	1957[b]
Production	51·3	49·1
of which factory	(24·0)	(31·9)
Construction	0·9	1·2
Transport	6·0	8·7
Commerce, food and services	27·0	24·1
Government and other	14·8	16·9
Total	100·0	100·0
Absolute total	1,253,326	2,418,000

SOURCES:
[a] Based on data from *Dai yonji zendōkyū daihyō taikai ni teishutsu seru Shanhai sōkōkai no hōkōsho* (Report from the General Labour Union of Shanghai on its activities: May 1926 to May 1927), translated into Japanese by Taicho Mikami and others (1962); Lieu, pp. 344 and 422; *CCCP* Ser. 10, No. 23, 8 Jun. 1950, p. 5.
[b] As Table 17.

in Shanghai between 1949 and 1957, and in some respects it has been possible to relate these to trends over the longer period from 1927.

Total employment between 1949 and 1957 grew at 1·2% per annum. In the same period the indigenous labour supply, net of those retained in the educational system, grew at 2·1%. This implies an increase in unemployment and for the whole period *net* employment opportunities created within the city were insufficient to absorb the *net* growth of the indigenous labour supply – although this was favourably affected by the growth of numbers retained in education.

Looking backwards, the overall employment growth rate of 1·2% may be compared with a pre-war long-run rate of 2·6%. Looking forwards, the rate of 1·2% must be seen in relation to a natural growth of population of 3·4%, since by the mid-1960s this would be the natural rate of increase of the labour supply. Clearly an acute employment crisis is indicated.

Our data on the labour supply enabled us to break down the components of supply in some detail. When this is done we find that the migrant component was only 17% which is far lower than the estimate of 44·5% for all urban areas made on the basis of Sung P'ing's

42

data. It is entirely possible that Shanghai's experience was of an exceptional character and that both estimates are accurate. An alternative possibility is that the official national data take insufficient account of the size of emigration – for in Shanghai it was the size of the outflows that reduced the net inflow to such modest proportions.

One very important implication of our population and employment data is that the proportion of non-productive dependants was growing in the cities throughout the whole period from the 1920s and that this trend accelerated during the 1950s. For as we show in the table below, the economically active proportion of the population fell in Shanghai from 47% in 1926/27, to 35·8% in 1957. This trend is explained in the 1950s by both the slow rate of growth of total employment and by the changing age structure of the urban population brought about by the rapid reduction in infant mortality. We lack official data on this, but our estimate is that the proportion of the Shanghai population under sixteen rose from 27% in 1930 to about 35% in 1957.[1]

Let us now consider the conclusions that can be drawn from our data on the structure of employment. From Table 16 it can be calculated that in 1957 production of all kinds accounted for nearly half of total employment, while industrial production accounted for 37·2%. This latter figure compares with a national average of 24·4%, which indicates the relative economic maturity of Shanghai.

Turning to the pre-war data, comparison with 1926/27 indicates that the relative importance of employment in *all* forms of production has remained about the same. This aggregate, however, conceals the accelerating growth of the *factory* sector and the comparative stagnation of traditional production. For over the whole period from 1929 to 1957, employment of workers and staff in factories grew at 3·3% per annum, and within this period the growth rate rose from 2·4% up to 1949, to 5·8% between 1949 and 1957.[2] The effect of

[1] Data for 1930 from *Statistics of Shanghai compiled in 1933* (1933), p. 3. 1957 data estimated by use of age structure data for 1949 and natural increase data as p. 33. Important additional information of the age structure of urban populations in the late 1950s is in 'The age structure of urban residents and urban development plans', *Ch'eng shih chien she* (Urban Construction, hereafter *CSCS*) 1957 No. 3, p. 5.
[2] 1929 data based on Lieu (1936), pp. 344 and 442; 1949 data from 'The development of the Shanghai textile industry', *CCCP* Ser. 10, No. 23, 8 Jun. 1950, p. 5; 1957 data as Table 17.

Table 20. *The employed population as a percentage of total population : national, Shanghai and other cities, pre-1937 and the late 1950s*

	pre-1937	late 1950s
National[a]	–	32·6
Canton[b]	39·3	25·0
Lushun-Dairen[c]	39·0	32·5
Nanking[d]	54·0	33·2
Shanghai[e]	47·0	35·8

SOURCES:

[a] Result of a national sample survey in 1956. 'The gap between the rise of living standards of peasants and workers is not great', *Ho nan jih pao* (Honan daily) 27 Sep. 1957.

[b] Data for 1928 in *Kuang chou shih cheng fu t'ung chi nien chien* (Statistical yearbook of the Canton City Government), (1929). Data for 1956 in 'A discussion of some problems of the peasants' standard of living', *NFJP* 13 Apr. 1957.

[c] Data for Dairen city in 1939 from Japanese sources quoted in Irene B. Taeuber, 'The demography of Chinese urbanisation: Kwantung and the South Manchurian Railway Zone', preliminary version of a paper read to a conference on *Urban society and political development in modern China* (1969). Later data for Lushun-Dairen, 'The standard of living of the city's workers and peasants is gradually rising', *Lü-Ta jih pao* (The Lushun-Dairen daily) 15 Jul. 1957.

[d] Data for Nanking in 1956 from *Statistical report on the population in Nanking City in 1936* (1937). Later data for Nanking and Wusih in 'A preliminary research survey into the difference in living standards of workers and peasants in Kiangsu province', *Lao tung* (Labour, hereafter *LT*) No. 21, 1957.

[e] Shanghai data from Tables 11, 17 and 20. Population data from Murphy, p. 22. Numerous sources suggest that 47% should be regarded as a minimum figure for participation in the pre-war period. For example, Yang Hsi-meng, *Shang hai kung jen sheng huo ch'eng tu ti i ko yen chiu* (Research into the standard of living of Shanghai workers), (1930).

this growth in the 1950s was to raise the share of factory employment from 24·1% in 1949 to 31·9% in 1957 and to provide 280,000 net new jobs.

Apart from industry the other dynamic sectors in the 1950s were health and government. Between 1949 and 1957 employment in these sectors grew at over 16% per annum and provided 247,000 net new jobs.[1]

We have no satisfactory measures of changes of employment in the traditional sector. In 1957 it accounted for 43·4% of all employ-

[1] Data for 1950 are from *Shang hai chieh fang i nien*, p. 80. Further confirmation of the small size of the pre-war urban bureaucracy is in Chu Pang-hsing and others, *Shang hai ch'an yeh yü Shang hai chih kung* (Shanghai industry and Shanghai workers and staff), (1937), chapter 24.

ment. In production it accounted for only a third of all employment and it seems likely that although there were some sharp fluctuations, the absolute level of employment remained fairly static. In the traditional commerce, transport and services sector, however, we think that there must have been substantial disabsorption. For comparison of the total net increase of employment and the net increase in industry, government and health, indicates that total disabsorption outside these sectors was 294,000 persons; in the light of fragmentary statistical evidence and significant qualitative information, it is certain that most of this must have been in traditional commerce, transport and services.[1] The implication of this is that these sectors must have declined absolutely in size by over 20%. Despite this our 1957 figure shows that the traditional commerce sector still accounted for 20% of all types of employment. The implication being that despite the rapid growth of industrial employment, strategies for employment had to take into account the employment effects in the traditional sector of any changes either in resource allocation or institutions.

In conclusion it is interesting to note that Shanghai's experience of sectoral employment change is quite different from that found in most developing countries in the post-war years. Industrial employment has grown much faster than in Latin America or countries such as India,[2] while traditional services, which elsewhere have been

[1] We have an employment series for services in the private sector which shows a decline from a peak of 40,950 in 1950 to 29,500 on the eve of socialisation in 1955. See, *Szu ying shang yeh ti she hui chu i kai tsao*, (*tzu liao*) (The socialist reform of private commerce (materials)), (1963), p. 323. Changes in the commerce sector are also hard to quantify, but the employment crisis in this sector in 1954 and 1955 confirms that a decline of employment was probable. An indication of the severity of this crisis is the fact that during the Shanghai reform of wholesale commerce between 1954 and 1955, of the 44,183 persons involved, 19,224 were neither absorbed into the reformed commerce system, nor found alternative employment, nor given any sort of re-training. See, *ibid.* p. 144. We also know that employment considerations were the prime factor in dictating *the tactics* of the socialisation of retail commerce in Shanghai; for it was argued that to 'allow the continued private management of the private retail commerce sector is very beneficial for the maintenance of employment', see, 'Why it is necessary to adopt different measures when implementing the socialist reform of private wholesale and retail commerce', *CFJP* 24 Mar. 1955.
[2] In India, the growth of factory employment between 1951 and 1961 was 2·97% per annum, *Handbook of labour statistics* (1965), table 1.8. In Latin America, the rate for the same period was 3·3%, 'Structural change in employment within the context of Latin America's economic development', *Economic bulletin for Latin America*, x, 1965 (1966), pp. 163–87.

an important factor in expanding urban employment, in Shanghai declined absolutely.[1] The one phenomenon that seems almost universal, is the rapid growth of modern bureaucratic employment.

EMPLOYMENT GROWTH IN OTHER CITIES

It is difficult to find official employment data for individual cities which are analytically useful – since even in the years in which economic data are generally plentiful, it was normal to describe employment achievements in terms of the gross number of persons for whom employment had been found. This figure therefore included persons returned to the countryside and persons for whom employment had been found in other cities and was gross of all employment losses. From the Bureaux' point of view, the use of this figure had the administrative advantage that it was easily extracted from their records, and there was the additional merit that, because the figure was gross, it was an attractive performance indicator at every level since it presented employment work in the most favourable possible light. For our purposes, however, such figures are of little value, since inter-area or inter-city variations in employment gains might well reflect variations in migration or the frequency of employment fluctuations, rather than long-run trends.

We have however some local data of value and these are reports of the growth of numbers of workers and staff which are shown in Table 21 below. These are reliable indicators of inter-area employment variations although it must be borne in mind that provincial data for *all* workers and staff do include some persons working in rural areas.

The data on industrial workers and staff are the most useful of all and these show marked regional variations of employment growth in the 1950s. Thus the provinces of Inner Mongolia, Kansu, Shensi and Kirin, all of which had several 'key-point' cities designated for rapid expansion, had employment growth rates double the national

[1] In Latin America 'miscellaneous services' had an employment growth rate between 1951 and 1961 of 4·7% per annum. This was substantially higher than the growth of factory employment. (See the article cited above.) The role of the service sector in Egyptian employment growth has been perceptively analysed by D.C. Mead, *Growth and structural change in the Egyptian economy* (1967), chapter 6.

Table 21. *Growth rates of population and workers and staff, 1949–57*

	All workers and staff, 1949–56/7	All workers and staff, 1952–56/7	Industrial workers and staff, 1949–56/7	Industrial workers and staff, 1952–56/7	Population, 1948/9–58
Canton (Mun.)[a]	—	8·8	—	7·9	4·9
Chengtu (Mun.)[b]	—	—	17·0	—	6·4
Chungking (Mun.)[c]	—	—	20·4	—	8·0
Harbin (Mun.)[d]	—	—	—	13·7	7·7
Heilungkiang (Prov.)[e]	—	—	—	—	—
Inner Mongolia (Auton. Region)[f]	18·7	—	23·7	—	2·0
Kansu (Prov.)[g]	—	17·1	—	17·1	11·9
Kirin (Prov.)[h]	—	—	—	16·2	—
Shanghai (Mun.)[i]	—	—	7·6	8·6	4·7
Shantung (Prov.)[j]	—	—	—	4·4	—
Shensi (Prov.)[k]	—	—	29·2	—	—
National[l]	15·0	9·2	12·6	8·5	7·1

(per cent per annum compound)

SOURCES:
[a] *KCJP* 29 Sep. 1957; Ullman, table 3, p. 35.
[b] *Ch'eng tu jih pao* (Chengtu daily) 11 Sep. 1957; Ullman, *ibid*.
[c] *Chung ch'ing jih pao* (Chungking daily) 12 Aug. 1957; Ullman, *ibid*.
[d] *Hei lung chiang jih pao* (Heilungkiang daily, hereafter *HLCJP*) 19 Dec. 1956.
[e] *HLCJP* 14 Aug. 1957.
[f] Estimates from *Nei Meng ku jih pao* (Inner Mongolia daily, hereafter *NMKJP*) 13 Apr. 1957 and *NMKJP* 26 Apr. 1957.
[g] *Kan su jih pao* (Kansu daily, hereafter *KSJP*) 26 Sep. 1957; *KSJP*, 10 Jul. 1957.
[h] *Chi lin jih pao* (Kirin daily, hereafter *CLJP*) 8 Dec. 1956.
[i] Data from p. 43, n. 2 and *HWP* 28 Dec. 1957.
[j] *Ta chung pao* (The masses daily) 3 Aug. 1957; Ullman, *ibid*.
[k] *Shan hsi jih pao* (Shensi daily, hereafter *SHJP*) 10 Jan. 1957.
[l] Emerson (1965), p. 128: 'Statistical materials on our country's population 1949–1956', *TCKT* 1957 No. 11, pp. 24–5; *Kuang ming jih pao* (The enlightenment daily), hereafter *KMJP*) 7 Oct. 1963.

average. In Shantung Province on the other hand, industrial employment grew at only half the national rate.

In using the employment data the fundamental limitation that has to be borne in mind is that although changes in workers and staff are meaningful indicators for inter-area comparison, they do not give a reliable indication of changes in the level of total employment. This is because total employment is not co-terminous with total numbers of workers and staff. This distinction is particularly important in older cities where the small-scale and traditional sectors are numerically important. In Canton, for example, total workers and staff accounted for about half, and industrial workers and staff for about one fifth of total employment.[1] Thus it is quite possible that rapid growth of workers and staff took place in a context of overall employment stagnation. This was actually the case in Shanghai where industrial workers and staff were growing in numbers by 7·6% per annum between 1949 and 1957, while total employment was only growing at 1·2% per annum. However, even allowing for this limitation, the data still suggest that the structural deficiency in the demand for labour indicated for Shanghai does not apply in key-point areas such as Kansu, Kirin and Inner Mongolia where very high employment absorption rates are indicated.

The population data in the final column reveal the range of demographic experience in the 1950s. Total urban population is seen to have been growing at 7·1% per annum and the data for Shanghai (4·7% per annum) and urban Kansu (11·9% per annum), reflect the demographic characteristics typical of new, key-point cities and the old treaty port cities respectively.

[1] *KCJP* 29 Sep. 1957; *KCJP* 13 Oct. 1957.

3

THE DETERMINANTS OF
STRUCTURAL EMPLOYMENT
CHANGE

THE DEMAND FOR LABOUR

The data in the last chapter leave much to be desired, but they all confirm the structural nature of the unemployment problem and suggest that by 1957 unemployment had reached high levels. In this chapter we shall attempt to summarise the causes of this although we shall leave discussion of the evolution of policy thinking until Part Two.

The main difficulty in making unemployment estimates was found to be the construction of satisfactory estimates of labour supply. The data on the demand side were more firmly based and these all confirm slow rates of overall employment growth, particularly after 1952. How can we explain this? Four factors seem important: the size and structure of the investment programme in the modern sector; the growth of labour productivity; the performance of the traditional sector; and the evolution of wages. Let us consider these in turn.

Investment and employment

The size of the modern sector investment programme was important because other things being equal this determined the growth of modern sector employment. The structure of the programme was relevant not only because of the employment implications of alternative inter-sectoral strategies, but also because choice of projects involved determining average capital intensity and gestation periods.

Up to the end of 1951 a flexible approach to the structure of industrial growth, and the availability of excess and slightly damaged capacity enabled the Government to keep investment costs low and gestation periods short. The result was high rates of growth of output

49

and employment in the industrial sector, which were reinforced by the effects of a generally favourable policy toward the private and traditional sectors. Emerson's data for industrial employment show that it grew at 22·6% between 1949 and 1952 and the Shanghai data also show 1949 and 1951 as years of fairly high absorption.[1]

The first three years of the First Plan, however, were marked by a sharp decline in absorption rates which contributed to a series of upheavals between 1956 and 1958. This decline was partly due to special factors that depressed activity, but was also related to the adoption of an investment strategy which, although ambitious in terms of the target rate of growth, involved concentration in sectors and projects where capital intensity was high and growing and where gestation periods were relatively long.[2] We are not concerned with the detailed argument behind this strategy here, but the main determinants of it were the character of the Sino-Russian economic aid agreement; the economic implications of the drive for autarchy and military strength; and the rationality of a policy which minimised indigenous skilled labour and management difficulties. Of these factors the latter was probably a good deal more important in deter-mining the actual outcome than has been realised. For we must remember that although the industrialisation debates of 1952–53 determined the plans for those years and the general character of the Plan for 1953–57, there was an area outside and supplementary to the main, 'key-point', projects where the usual explanations of capital intensity were not necessarily applicable. Yet even in these areas the drive to capital intensity is visible. An interesting example of this is the construction industry, in which capital intensity doubled between 1953 and 1955 while numbers employed declined abso-

---

[1] See Chapter 1, Table 8, Chapter 4, Table 31.

[2] In 1952, capital intensity in the light and heavy sectors of industry was approximately the same. By 1955, data suggests that capital intensity in the eight main heavy sectors had increased by over 50%, whereas the increase in the paper and cotton industries (taken as representative of light industry), was only 7%. See, 'The technical level of our country's industrial output', *HHPYK* 1957 No. 12, p. 115. Gestation periods in light industry were much shorter than in the heavy sector. Typical heavy sector projects were estimated to have gestation periods of three to four years compared to between one and two years for light industry investments. For heavy sector data see, 'Livelihood must be subordinated to the development of production', *WHP* 17 Dec. 1953. For light industry see, Hu Ming, 'Dig out the potential in light industry', *CHCC* 1956 No. 5, pp. 8–11.

lutely – leading to identifiable unemployment of skilled workers about which the authorities were very concerned. Yet this increase in capital intensity cannot be wholly explained in terms of Soviet influence, technological standards set in the defence sector, inflexible complementarities, etc. Indeed, construction is an industry where the possibilities for varying capital intensity are considerable, and since unemployment was a problem of particular seriousness during 1954–55, the policy of capital substitution seems extraordinary. It is possible that humanitarian factors entered into it, since some construction tasks are extremely unpleasant without a degree of mechanisation. But it can be argued that the main drive for mechanisation in construction came from cadres who were faced with labour management problems of such peculiar difficulty that capital substitution made sense. For to the planners and these cadres, physical plan fulfilment ranked higher than planning objectives intended to minimise costs or optimise factor use – thus it was rational for these cadres to violate narrow economic rationality in favour of broader organisational considerations, and it was rational for the planners to tolerate this.[1]

Although the First Plan investment strategy was basically adhered to, in the latter part of the Plan period it was subject to two important modifications of relevance to employment. In 1956 there was a revision of the inter-sectoral investment allocation in favour of light industry which had favourable implications for employment absorption because of the lower capital intensity and shorter gestation periods in this sector. Then in 1957, the annual investment plan laid new emphasis on the importance of diverting resources to small-scale enterprises using more labour-intensive techniques of production – even if this involved loss of quality of output, loss of face for cadres managing enterprises which did not meet the full requirements of modernity, and by implication, loss of re-investible surplus per unit of capital. The 1957 Plan was therefore the first occasion on which the investment plan for the modern sector was explicitly modified for employment reasons.

---

[1] 'The basic situation in our country's construction industry', *TCKT* 1956 No. 24, pp. 31–3. 'Strive to do labour assignment work well in 1955', *LT* 1955 No. 1, pp. 13–14, and 'Important tasks in current labour assignment work', *LT* 1955 No. 8, pp. 4–5.

Productivity and employment

Let us now consider the effects of productivity growth on employment absorption. Productivity is closely related to capital intensity, and the relationships between industrial output, labour, capital and productivity at the national level during the First Five Year Plan period are set out in Tables 22 and 23. In Table 22 the data take the form of indexes and in Table 23, the indexes of output, labour and capital are converted into growth rates and two estimates are made of the productivity residual by using alternative weightings for capital and labour.

Table 22. *Indexes of industrial output, labour, capital, 1952–57 (national)*

	(1952 = 100) 1957
Output	209·6
Labour	149·5
Capital	231·9
Capital per head	155·1
Output per head	140·2
Output per unit of capital	90·5

SOURCES:
National data are from Michael Field, 'Labor productivity in industry', in Alexander Eckstein, Walter Galenson and Ta-chung Liu, *Economic trends in Communist China* (1968), Tables 3 and 7.

In these tables, output growth is seen to be the result of capital, labour and productivity growth (as measured by the residual). Capital intensity and output per man are shown to have risen, while output per unit of capital fell slightly. For us, the main implication is that at the aggregate level productivity had an adverse effect on employment absorption during the First Five Year Plan. From the planners point of view this may have been perfectly rational – taking into account the cost of additional employment and the relationship between this and the savings generated in the industrial sector. For if it is the case that for a planned level of output there is some area of choice between additional employment and additional productivity, the planners will choose that combination of the two which equalises their valuation of the savings made possible by additional productivity and the social benefits of the additional employment generated. In terms of employment this involves a choice between the present and the future; for the more employment is increased immediately, the less savings there will be to increase future employment through capital formation. In general, the Chinese planners seem to have had a preference for productivity over employment and the long run over the short.

Table 23. *Growth rates of industrial output, labour, capital and productivity, 1952–57 (national)*

	(per cent per annum)
Output	16·0
Labour	8·45
Capital	18·33
Labour and capital	11·42
Residual	4·58 or 2·49

SOURCE: As Table 22.
The two weightings used here to calculate the productivity residual are:
(*a*) The 'arbitrary' weightings ($L = 0·7$ $K = 0·3$) used by T.C. Liu to estimate the Domestic Product productivity residual and (*b*) Eckstein's estimate of the proportion that the industrial wage bill bears to the net product of industry ($L = 0·487$ $K = 0·513$). The latter seems the more logical, although it may be noted that Liu's weighting may not be so arbitrary after all, since it is so close to the labour/capital share of the European and American national incomes. T.C. Liu in *The profile*, pp. 62–3; Alexander Eckstein, *The national income of Communist China* (1961), p. 79; Edward F. Denison, *Why growth rates differ: post-war experience in nine western countries* (1967).

These national data are a useful indication of the way in which employment and productivity growth were related in the industrialisation of the First Five Year Plan. However the data do conceal regional variations which are important if the character of this industrialisation process is to be properly understood. For on the one hand there were cities in which the sources of growth were predominantly employment and productivity increases, whereas in others growth was due mainly to increases of capital and employment. We may characterise these growth processes as *Shanghai* and *key-point* growth respectively; in Table 24 below we illustrate the difference between these with data for the city of Shanghai and the province of Kansu – which is dominated by the city of Lanchow. The contrast between these two types of growth is important. In Shanghai, we have a process that may be described as growth without investment in which the sources of increased output are almost

Table 24. *Growth rates of industrial output, labour, capital and productivity in the industrial sector of Shanghai city and Kansu Province, 1952–57*

	(per cent per annum) Shanghai	Kansu
Output	14·17	30·9
Labour	8·59	17·1
Capital	0·79	43·1
Labour and capital	6·25	24·03
Residual[a]	9·58	0·4

[a] Estimated using method (*b*) in Table 23.

SOURCES:
Shanghai data from 'Total output doubled in five years', *HWJP* 28 Dec. 1957. Kansu data from 'Construction achievements tremendous; the people's livelihood rising', *KSJP* 5 Jul. 1957; 'The city of Lanchow advances on the road to industrialisation', *KSJP* 17 Jul. 1957; *KSJP* 26 Sep. 1957; *KSJP* 12 Jun. 1958. Total employment of workers and staff has been used as a proxy for industrial workers and staff. In this case the procedure is reasonable since we know that in Lanchow city (which accounted for half of total employment in Kansu), industrial workers and staff were 86% of all workers and staff.

entirely labour and productivity – the increase in the latter being so great that although Shanghai had only a very small increase in capital (while the national stock doubled), the city achieved output and employment growth rates about two-thirds as large as the national average. How was this done? How was it possible to add increasing quantities of labour to a fixed stock of capital and simultaneously achieve a considerable increase in productivity? It seems probable that apart from the effects of recovery from a position of excess capacity, three techniques were consciously used: increasing utilisation of capacity through the extension of shift work on the basis of an eight hour system; increasing intensity of work; and improved rationality of labour utilisation.[1]

One immediate result of analysing the sources of Shanghai's growth is that when we take into account the lack of capital formation in the 1950s the growth of output and employment in this period becomes more impressive by comparison with pre-1949 years than would otherwise be the case. And although it must be borne in mind that the wartime period in Shanghai was a period of sharp fluctuations, capital removals and replacements, etc., the data are worth inspection and are shown in Table 25.

Growth of the type experienced in Shanghai in the 1950s has some impressive aspects; the snag is that it is not self-sustaining. For without additional investment there will come a point when output and employment growth will slow dramatically. Output growth will slow when the possibilities for increasing the utilisation of plant have been exhausted and again if campaigns to increase labour intensity have diminishing returns. Employment growth is also bound to be checked when the limits of plant utilisation through shift work are reached – unless the planners are prepared to multiply the number of shifts purely as a device to increase employment. Since employment expansion of this kind would be at the expense of labour productivity – increases of which the Chinese planners valued highly – it seems improbable that employment growth of this kind would be tolerated for very long.

The contrast between Shanghai and the key-point province of Kansu as shown in Table 24 is striking.[2] In Kansu, industrialisation

[1] The cotton-spinning industry is an example of the degree of increased capital utilisation in Shanghai in the 1950s. Between 1949 and 1956, the number of spindles installed actually declined by 3% while output rose by 114%. Data on spindles in 'Make further use of the potential of Shanghai's textile industry', *CFJP* 13 Aug. 1956 and *CFJP* 22 Aug. 1956. Output data is from, *Wo kuo kang t'ieh tien li mei t'an chi hsieh fang chih tsao chih kung yeh ti chin hsi* (Our country's iron and steel, electric power, coal, machinery, textile and paper industries – past and present, hereafter *Wo kuo*), (1958), chapter 5.

[2] An incomplete list of 'key-point' cities published in 1957 included the following: Anshan (Liaoning Pr.); Chengchow (Honan Pr.); Chengtu (Szechuan Pr.); Harbin (Kirin Pr.); Kirin (Kirin Pr.); Lanchow (Kansu Pr.); Loyang (Honan Pr.); Paotou (Inner Mongolian Autonomous Region); Peking (Hopei Pr.); Shenyang (Liaoning Pr.); Sian (Shensi Pr.); Taiyuan (Shansi Pr.); Tatung (Shansi Pr.); Tsitsierhbin (Heilungkiang Pr.). See Chang Yen-hsing, 'The work of urban construction must be arranged in conformity with the policy of building up the nation economically', *CHCC* 1957 No. 12, p. 4.

started in 1949 from the very small base of 39 factories (compared with 12,570 in Shanghai in the same year). Capital accumulation in Kansu however was astonishingly rapid – probably slightly above 30% per annum compound for the whole period up to 1957 and

Table 25. *The growth of industrial output, employment and capital in Shanghai, 1933–57*

	(per cent per annum)	
	1933–49	1949–57
Output	3·4[a]	18·1[d]
Employment	1·8[b]	5·8[e]
Capital	4·0[c]	nil[f]
Residual	0·47	15·27

SOURCES:

[a] This estimate is based on data for electricity output and involves the assumptions that the pre-war relationship between electricity and industrial output held in the post-war period, and that the national relationship between generating capacity and electricity output between 1936 and 1949 held in Shanghai. *Ten great years*, p. 91; *Wo kuo*, chapter 2; Ch'en Chen, *Chung Kuo chin tai kung yeh shih tzu liao* (Materials on the modern industrial history of China), Vol. 4 (1961), pp. 881–94; Wu Yuan-li, *Economic development and the use of energy resources in Communist China* (1963), chapter 2. The use of energy data as indicator of economic change is discussed in A.G. Frank, 'Industrial capital stocks and energy consumption', *Economic journal*, March 1959, pp. 170–4 and J.C. Warren Jr. 'Energy and economic advance', *The Philippine economic journal*, 1st Semester, 1964, pp. 78–87.
[b] Based on sources in Chapter 2, pp. 43–4.
[c] This is a crude estimate based on the growth of electricity generating capacity and the number of spindles installed in cotton spinning factories. Electricity data as note [a]; spindle data Yen Chung-p'ing *Chung Kuo chin tai ching chi shih t'ung chi tzu liao hsü chi* (Selected statistics of China's modern economic history), (1955), pp. 109–10.
[d] Chapter 1, Table 2.
[e] Chapter 2, p. 43.
[f] In Table 24 we estimated that capital accumulation during the First Plan was small but positive. In the pre-plan period however there were removals of capital equipment from Shanghai to cities less vulnerable to air attack from Taiwan. We therefore think that on balance there was no net investment in the whole period 1949–57, although there was investment in some sectors – for example cotton weaving.

over 43% per annum in the First Plan. This rapid accumulation generated employment growth in the First Plan of 17·1% per annum. According to our estimates, however, the productivity residual in Kansu was only just positive and was far lower than in Shanghai. Thus one conclusion that can be drawn is that if Kansu was typical it appears that in key-point cities Chinese industrial growth was not as dissimilar from the low productivity, explosive growth of the early Russian plans as comparison of aggregate Russian and Chinese data would suggest.[1]

Employment in the traditional sector

We have now to consider the extent to which the employment problems implicit in the strategy of the First Plan were alleviated by the employment performance in the non-industrial sectors, i.e. traditional production and commerce and the Government sector. The data in the second chapter suggest that of these only the last showed any sign of significant expansion while the traditional sector experienced substantial disabsorption. The importance of this for urban employment is indicated by the fact that even in Shanghai, which had an industrial sector of above average size, in 1957 the traditional sector still accounted for 40% of all employment, and data which show the minute size of the modern industrial sector in Canton and Peking (Table 26) confirm that in other cities it must have been at least equally important.

Table 26. *Industrial employment as a percentage of total employment and population in Shanghai, Canton, Peking and all urban areas, 1931–57*

	1931	1949	1954	1957
as a percentage of population				
Shanghai	7	10	—	11
Canton	—	—	6	7
Peking	—	3·4	—	—
All urban areas	—	5·3	—	8
as a percentage of all employment				
Shanghai	14	23	—	32
Canton	—	—	—	20
All urban areas	—	—	—	24·4

SOURCES:
Shanghai, based on data cited in Chapter 2.
Canton, estimate based on data in *NFJP* 12 Dec. 1955; *KCJP* 13 Oct. 1957; *TKP* (Hong Kong) 1 Jan. 1957; *WHP* (Hong Kong) 4 Feb. 1957; *Kuang chou shih cheng fu t'ung chi nien chien.*
Peking data, *JMJP* 17 Nov. 1949.
National data, data cited in Chapters 1, Table 8 and Chapter 2, Table 21.

[1] See Chapter 6, pp. 102–3.

The poor employment performance of the traditional sector was due both to a fundamental hostility to private and small-scale activity and to the fact that the expansion of these sectors led to general loss of control and the diversion of resources from investment and the public sector to consumption and the private sector. During the First Plan period, the fulfilment of the plan for the public sector was given priority, irrespective of the implications of this for the traditional and small scale sector and for consumption and urban employment.

Apart from disabsorption, another effect of pressure on the traditional sector must have been an increase in frictional unemployment – both rural and urban – since the traditional sector (particularly commerce) has long acted in China as a mechanism for equilibrating labour market pressures in these sectors. The slight capital requirements necessary to participate in traditional occupations have always made entry and exit easy for those able to alternate between agricultural and non-agricultural occupations. Such alteration might or might not require migration, and could be either seasonal or motivated either by fluctuations in the non-agricultural sector, or, more frequently, by catastrophes in agriculture. In the latter case, employment switching offered an efficient way of minimising unemployment and sharing available urban income. This sort of process was certainly known in the nineteenth century, can be observed in the 1930s and was still in evidence in the 1950s.[1]

[1] It was said in the mid-nineteenth century that, 'when the profits of commerce are small, those who plough and weave will be numerous'; Mary C. Wright, *The last stand of Chinese conservatism: the T'ung Chih restoration, 1862–1874* (1957), p. 156. There is a vivid account of occupation switching in the Hangchow area in 1931 in *Hang chou shih ching chi tiao ch'a* (An economic survey of Hangchow), (1932). This report described how bankruptcy and natural disasters forced many peasants into the city where they participated in rickshaw, construction and commerce work. The report also showed how problems were arising because numbers employed in the commerce sector were increasing *without* there being any increase of trade to justify them.

For the 1950s, an instructive account of the role of the handicraft industry in a small town is 'An introduction to, and some views on the handicraft industry in Ocheng' (Hupeh), *LT* 1954 No. 3, This report described the way in which the handicraft labour force fluctuated in response to the agricultural cycle. Over half of the labour force owned land and almost all the rest assisted in agricultural work whenever labour requirements were especially high. The writer went on to show how lack of working capital from public sources and rigid employment administration were hampering handicraft employment which was vital to local income and employment.

Employment and wages

There are two important aspects of the relationship between wages and employment in our period. First, the size of urban wage differentials indicate that some urban groups must have been earning wages that took them above subsistence, and the implication of this is that wage policy and administration were responsible for constricting both immediate and long-term employment opportunities; immediate constriction because differentials absorbed resources that could have been used to expand employment in work with slight or no new capital requirements; longer term constriction because differentials absorbed resources that could have been used for investment and the expansion of future employment.[1]

This aggregate relationship between wage differentiation, the wage bill and the level of urban employment was explicitly recognised in 1957 when it was used as part of the theoretical case for a policy of systematic wage reduction.[2]

The second point about the wage-employment relationship is that it had particular importance for the private sector – since wage rises in the public sector were reflected in pressures on the private sector to keep pace. In the upswings, these pressures on the private sector worked through a market mechanism when the private sector competed openly with the public sector for urban labour. In the slack years, the pressure came from unions and groups of political activists within enterprises, who were acting on Party instructions to intensify financial pressures on the private sector with a view to encouraging 'requests' for socialisation.

These policies and pressures were undoubtedly a serious problem for enterprises whose viability was dependent on maintaining wage

[1] We know that minimum wages in the modern sector were fixed at levels sufficient to maintain two adults in urban conditions and that the range of occupational differentials was such that the rate for skilled workers in industry in the top grade was approximately 2·5 to 3 times the rate for the bottom grade. Apart from occupational and inter-industry differentials in the modern sector, there were substantial inter-sector differentials. For example, the average monthly income of workers and staff in the modern sector in Shanghai was up to three times the average earnings of people in the traditional sector. Wang Ya-chiang, *Kung yeh ch'i yeh kung tzu li lun yü shih chien* (The theory and practice of wages in industrial enterprises), (1955); *HWJP* 2 Sep. 1957; *HWJP* 19 Jan. 1957; *JMJP* 19 Aug. 1957.
[2] Sung P'ing 'Why we must implement the rational low wage system', *Hsüeh hsi* (Study, hereafter *HH*) 1957 No. 23, pp. 14–17.

levels below those in modern, public sector enterprises. Again, this was periodically recognised, notably in 1954, when there was a vigorous campaign to reduce wages in the traditional sector to stimulate employment.[1] Over the whole period however, wage pressures must have played an important part in the employment disabsorption in the private and traditional sectors.

THE SUPPLY OF LABOUR

In this section we analyse the determinants of the supply of job seekers in the urban labour market. The two factors of particular importance are participation rates and migration. Population changes due to changes in vital rates are not relevant here since the population acceleration of the 1950s was only of direct significance for labour supply in the 1960s.

Participation

The three important aspects of participation are: time worked; age limits; and the degree of female participation in the labour force. The data on these subjects are incomplete but we have sufficient to indicate that radical changes took place between 1930 and 1957.

By comparison with the pre-war period, hours worked were certainly reduced in the 1950s. A survey of factories in Shanghai in 1930 showed that, on average, workers were employed for ten hours a day. And although in 1950 it was said that an eight hour day was not an immediate possibility, by the mid-1950s such a day was normal in the modern sector. The effect of this reduction in hours was to increase opportunity for participation for the labour force.[2]

National data on the age composition of the urban labour force are only available in the 1955 State Statistical Bureau survey of workers and staff in public sector industry and construction. The results of this survey are in Table 27 below.

The implication of this survey is that in these sectors participation was effectively limited to those between eighteen and sixty years of

[1] 'Wage adjustment in handicraft production cooperatives during the past year', *Chung yang ho tso t'ung hsiun* (The central cooperative bulletin) 11 Dec. 1954, pp. 13-14.
[2] See *Statistics of Shanghai compiled in 1933*, table 3, p. 3, and further discussion of this in Chapter 5.

age. But we think that this has to be subject to some modification at both ends before it can be applied to all urban employment. For example there is substantial evidence of failure to retire in some industries, and in the traditional and small scale sectors (where the retirement regulations did not have the force of law) it seems probable that the upper limit of the official participation rate was in practice very flexible.[1] At the lower end, there is no evidence that

Table 27. *The age structure of workers and employees in public sector industry and capital construction in 1955*

Age	(%)
under 18	1·0
18–25	38·3
26–35	35·9
36–45	17·1
46–50	4·3
51–55	2·2
56–60	0·9
over 60	0·3
Total	100·0%

SOURCE:
'The number, structure, and distribution of workers and staff in the whole country in 1955', *TCKT* 1956, No. 23, pp. 28–30.

those who failed to move into the senior stream of the Middle School system at sixteen were debarred from employment when they could obtain it. But it is clear from the evidence of our table that up to 1955 only a small proportion of the younger age group managed to get into the public sector. This is not surprising, since competition to get into the public sector was very fierce, and in most branches of it preference would be given to persons with some skill or experience.

We have no national figures on the age structure of the pre-war urban labour force but Shanghai data on the factory labour force all indicate that it was very young. For example a survey of the age structure in a cotton textile factory produced the results shown in Table 28.

[1] 'The key to fulfilling the labour plan for 1957', *LT* 1957 No. 3, pp. 2–3.

Comparison of these figures with the national data for the late 1950s underlines the importance of the elimination of child labour on the age structure of the urban labour force and implies a substantial increase in labour force participation prospects for people who were within the official age limits.

Turning now to the question of female participation we are again thrown back on the Shanghai data and in Tables 29 and 30 we have figures for female participation in the total and factory labour force.

Table 28. *The age structure of workers in a Shanghai textile mill in the late 1920s*

Age	(%)
10	0·05
11–15	23·02
16–20	36·17
21–25	19·93
26–30	12·11
31–40	7·2
41–50	1·15
51–55	0·37
Total	100·0

SOURCE:
H.D. Fong, *Cotton industry and trade in China* (1932), p. 116.

The significance of these materials is that they suggest that by shortening hours, by abolishing child labour, and by limiting female participation to a lower share of employment than in the pre-war period, the labour administrators were able to mitigate substantially the effects of low employment absorption rates on open male unemployment – although in the nature of the case this was largely a once for all process.

For Table 30 shows that in 1931 women and children accounted for 61% of the factory labour force in Shanghai. Yet by 1957, this figure had dropped to 45% of a much enlarged labour force. The pre-war proportion of females in the total labour force is not known, but it must certainly have been higher than the 21% estimated to have been in it in 1957.

Finally, the one other factor bearing on effective participation in the labour force is the educational retention. The impact of this in the case of Shanghai was estimated in our second chapter, and the national data on which this estimate was based show that during the First Five Year Plan the annual net inflow into the educational system was equal to 20·1% of the annual indigenous entry into the

Table 29. *Females as a percentage of the total employed labour force in Shanghai in 1957*

1931	1949/50	1957
–	–	21

SOURCE: 'Half a million Shanghai women and girls participate in construction', *WHP* 8 Mar. 1957.

Table 30. *Females and children as a percentage of the factory labour force in Shanghai, 1931–57*

	1931	1957
Females	51[a]	45[b]
Children	10	—

SOURCES:
[a] Lieu (1936), p. 228.
[b] 'Childbirth must be planned', *HWJP* 3 Jan. 1957.

urban labour force. The problem was, as we shall see later, that the favourable impact of the educational system on the labour supply depended on a rate of educational expansion which could not be steadily maintained in the long run.

Migration

Migration was the second major factor bearing on the urban labour supply. Internal migration has a long history in China and satisfactory accounts of it are scarce. In this section we can do no more than try to identify those aspects of the migrations of the 1950s that are relevant to the analysis of employment change and policy.

Migrations in the 1950s were of many types. The distance involved, for example, varied enormously. In 1957 (when migration reached a peak) it was reported that some groups of people were moving from one end of China to the other. The more characteristic migration, however, was that involving movement between cities and their fairly immediate hinterland. Thus most migrants to Shanghai came from the East China provinces of Kiangsu, Chekiang and Anhui. It should be noted moreover, that in the urban suburbs the distinction between the urban and rural area is mainly administrative.

In the urban suburbs, factories are placed in the middle of paddy fields and urban workers have small plots on which they cultivate vegetables. Thus peasants may participate in factory or construction work and workers engage in cultivation without physical migration; and frequently, prior to 1956, families divided their labour between agricultural and non-agricultural occupations. This interpenetration of the rural and urban areas caused many peculiar problems in city administration (notably in the implementation of land reform), and in considering the problems of controlling population and labour force movements it has always to be borne in mind.[1]

A third point worth remembering when analysing the migrations of the 1950s, is that seasonal migration and movement in response to agricultural catastrophe has had a long history in traditional China, and that there was a precedent for economically motivated, long-term migration on a massive scale in the period between 1912 and 1949. During this period, although fear of banditry and the consequences of war were important motives for movement, the economic attractions of Manchuria and the Treaty Port towns were increasingly important.[2]

[1] The phenomenon of families dividing their labour between sectors was known in the pre-war period in Shanghai. Young girls often walked up to two hours a day between their family homes in the suburbs and the cotton mills. H.D. Lamson, 'The effect of industrialization upon village livelihood', *Chinese economic journal*, October 1931, pp. 1025–82. The Shanghai land reform is analysed (by implication) in *The Shanghai City Government methods for implementing land reform in the Shanghai suburbs, Hua Tung ch'ü ts'ai cheng ching chi fa ling hui pien* (Compendium of economic and financial regulations for the East China Military Region), (1951), pp. 2008–15.

[2] Murphy, chapter 2, also Robert W. Barnett, *Economic Shanghai: hostage to politics 1937–1941* (1941), chapter II. The final stage of the civil war also led to a general migration into the cities. Jean Chesneaux, 'Notes sur l'evolution recente de l'habitat

The effects of these migrations were particularly visible in pre-war Manchuria and in Shanghai. In Shanghai, surveys conducted in the late 1920s and 1930s all showed that the city's population and labour force were predominantly non-Shanghaiese in origin and that migration was increasingly motivated by economic considerations. After 1937, however, the Sino-Japanese war became the major influence on migration and many Shanghai workers moved out either to the Communist areas in the North or to the Nationalist areas in the West.[1]

The scale of migration after 1949

Let us now consider the scale on which migrations took place after 1949 and their impact on population and labour force changes in urban areas. The only national data available state that there was a rural–urban migration during the First Plan period of 8,000,000 persons which accounts for 29% of total urban population growth during that period.[2] This is the figure used by Emerson to estimate that migration accounted for 44% of the net addition to the urban labour force.

The local data are more specific and interesting than this. We estimated in Chapter 2 that in Shanghai net migration accounted for 33·6% of population growth between 1949 and 1957 and 17% of the addition to the supply of job seekers in the same period. We have other data for Canton and Peking. In Canton, migration was reported to have accounted for 43% of total population growth while in Peking, migrants accounted for 70% of population growth between 1949 and 1957.[3] These data illustrate our point about the variety of

urbaine en Asie', *L'information geographique*, 13 (1949), pp. 169–75, and 14 (1950), pp. 1–8. Helpful accounts of the migration to Manchuria in the 1920s arc in *The Manchuria year book*, 1932/33, pp. 439–63; George Babcock Cressey, *China's geographic foundations* (1934), pp. 222–6; F.C. Jones, *Manchuria since 1931* (R.I.I.A. (O.U.P.): 1949), chapter IX; Waller Wynne Jr. *The population of Manchuria* (1958), p. 20.

[1] In 1930, a survey showed that only 26% of the total population of Shanghai had been born in the city, and that of the rest, 40% had come from Kiangsu and 20% from Chekiang, *Statistics of Shanghai compiled in 1933*, table 5, p. 4. In the factory studied by Kuo Heng-shih in Kunming, 30 out of 63 skilled workers had come from Shanghai. Kuo Heng-shih, *China enters the machine age* (Harvard University Press: 1944).

[2] Sung P'ing, 'Let's discuss the problem of employment', *HH* No. 12, 18 Jun. 1957, p. 26.

[3] Estimates for Canton from 'Kwangtung's population has increased by 31% in the past seven years', *WHP* 3 Apr. 1957; 'Canton establishes an office', *WHP* (Hong Kong)

China's demographic experience and it is interesting to note that migration was a particularly important component of population growth in the key-point city of Peking. This suggests that migration was probably also of great importance in the new cities of the North West such as Sian and Lanchow.

Apart from the question of scale, the outstanding feature of migration data is the picture of population mobility presented. In Shanghai, gross immigration was nearly two and a half times as great as the final net figure; and the gross addition to the labour force was more than four times the net addition. This tremendous mobility is confirmed by a remarkable survey of population change in three sample residential districts in Shanghai in 1954 and 1955.[1] This survey showed that in these two years, 35% and 43% respectively of the total population were involved in migration of some sort. In one area, in 1955, the figure was 74%. It is true that some of this migration must have been intra-city movement, but we can surmise from other materials that a great deal of it involved movement to or from rural areas. Two conclusions appear warranted by this. First, despite the imposition of severe formal restrictions, population mobility was probably as high in the mid-1950s as it had been in the Greater Shanghai area in the early 1930s.[2] Second, if the authorities had not been able to reverse rural–urban flows to the extent that they did, the unemployment problem would have been very much more serious than was actually the case.

The motives for migration

Motives for migration in the 1950s were similar to those operating in the pre-1949 period, except that the upheavals of rural reorganisation replaced war and banditry as the most important non-economic factor in the migration decision. Up to 1957, seasonal migrations based on the agricultural cycle and the requirements of the construction and other seasonal industries, continued as in the pre-1949

9 Dec. 1958; 'This year 100,000 surplus population to be mobilised to return to rural production', *KCJP* 15 Feb. 1958. Peking data from 'The urban population must be controlled', *JMJP* 27 Nov. 1957.

[1] 'Experience and a simple example of the analysis of fluctuating population birth rates', *TCKT* 1957 No. 6, pp. 25–7.

[2] In 1932, total migrations in and out of Greater Shanghai were 672,000 in a population of 1,580,000. *Statistics of Shanghai compiled in 1933*, table 1, p. 1 and table 7, p. 6.

period.[1] Similarly, natural disasters remained as a stimulant to movement into the urban areas. For example, the influxes of 1954/55 and 1957 were all related to natural disasters, although these combined with other factors to make migrations exceptionally large. One difference between migration in response to disasters in the pre- and post-1949 periods may have been that in the latter, migrations initially prompted by disaster were often irreversible, whereas traditionally peasants returned to the countryside after the catastrophe had subsided.[2]

Turning now to the long-run forces behind urban immigration we find that one of the most important was the pressure on land in the immediate urban hinterland which was a result of population growth, industrialisation, and rehousing. We have some evidence for the growth of such pressures in Shanghai and Canton and a particularly striking example of the problem is the experience of the city of Foochow.[3] In the Foochow suburbs at the time of the land reform a population of 115,000 peasants worked 7,040 hectares of land. By 1956, the rural population had grown by 25% while the arable area had shrunk by 7% due to absorption of land for industrial and residential use.

This pressure on land in the urban hinterland may well have been part of a broader process which explains migration from the rural areas. For many reports state that landlessness was an important factor in migration, particularly after the land reforms of 1949 to 1952 and as a result of the polarisation of wealth in the rural areas in 1954 and 1955. It must also have contributed to pressure on rural employment, food and income, each of which played an identifiable part in pushing peasants towards the cities.

[1] A report from Anshan in January 1953 indicated that the huge migration then taking place was in fact an intensification of customary, slack season migration. 'The People's Government in Fei Tung county should persuade peasants that they ought not to blindly migrate to the towns', *JMJP* 30 Jan. 1953; see also 'Stop blind migration to the towns, *Fu chien jih pao* (Fukien daily, hereafter *FCJP*) 24 Mar. 1957, in which the problem of stopping long established seasonal migrations is discussed.

[2] 'Mobilise peasants from outside to return to the countryside and participate in spring ploughing', *CFJP* 10 Mar. 1957. This article brings out the way in which natural disasters, the collectivisation and the income attraction of cities could combine to bring about a migration decision.

[3] 'The built up area of Shanghai enlarged by half', *HWJP* 8 Aug. 1957; 'The economic geography of Canton City', *Ti li hsüeh tzu liao* (Geographical study materials) 1958 No. 3, pp. 118–28; 'Develop production and arrange employment', *FCJP* 15 May 1957.

The problems of rural employment require deep and separate investigation which we have not been able to give them.[1] But the evidence for rural unemployment, at least of a seasonal variety, is strong, and prior to 1956 the search for employment was one of the most frequently given reasons for the rural–urban migrations. One interesting aspect of this is that agricultural reorganisation in the early and mid-1950s tended to aggravate the problem; for we often find it said that the generation of unemployment by Mutual Aid Teams and Low Level Cooperatives was one of the main causes of their instability, and not infrequently of their total collapse.[2] The problem of rural unemployment seems to have been particularly intractable in the densely populated region of East China. The Foochow material referred to earlier, for example, states that some cooperatives in the Foochow suburbs had less than 0·0067 of a hectare per head, with the result that the demand for work (and thereby income), required elaborate arrangements for task rotation and led to violence among the peasantry.

Food and income played a predictably important role in stimulating migration. For although there are substantial variations in agricultural income in the different regions, in many areas, notably the North China plain and parts of East China, the structural deficiencies of agriculture were reflected in low incomes. Apart from the low level of incomes, there was the factor of uncertainty. Uncertainty is unavoidable in an unmechanised agriculture in a country with the climatic characteristics of China, but it was accentuated in the 1950s both by variations in taxation policy and by collectivisation drives of unpredictable outcome.

Finally, one point that is often overlooked in discussion of the material incentives for migration is that income changes, actual and

[1] Examples of analyses of rural employment in areas of North and South China are, 'Ying Kou County, Sung Kiang District solves the problem of surplus labour in agricultural co-operatives', *Liao ning jih pao* (Liaoning daily, hereafter *LNJP*) 20 Nov. 1954, and 'Where is the outlet for surplus labour power?' *NFJP* 19 Nov. 1956.

[2] *FCJP* 26 Apr. 1952; *FCJP* 23 May 1952; *FCJP* 24 Jun. 1952. 'Take rural surplus labour and use it for land improvement', *Chung ch'ing hsin hua jih pao* (Chunking New China daily, hereafter *CCHHJP*) 26 Oct. 1952. 'Seriously regard and solve the problem of surplus labour within the mutual aid team', *Hsin hu nan pao* (New Hunan daily, hereafter *HHNP*) 16 Apr. 1954, and 'Stop peasants blindly infiltrating cities', *Shan t'ou jih pao* (Swatow daily, hereafter *STJP*) 22 Jan. 1957.

promised, were effective causes of both urban immigration and emigration. This was particularly the case in the years 1955–57 which we shall be examining in more detail later. In Shanghai for example the good harvest of 1955 and the promise of high incomes after the High Tide of Socialism, greatly facilitated the return of 500,000 peasants to the rural areas in mid-1955. Conversely, it was the failure of agricultural incomes to satisfy the expectations of the newly cooperativised peasants which in late 1956 and 1957, lead to an uncontrollable return to the city.[1]

The material push from the rural areas and the real and apparent economic attractions of the cities were by no means the only influences on migration in the 1950s. We have to make allowance also for the tremendous impact, particularly on the young, of the vision of China's future which was propagated in the early 1950s. This vision was dominated by the related concepts of the Party, the industrial worker and the city, and in some ways it confirmed prejudices against rural life inherited from the intelligentsia of traditional China. By the mid-1950s the inappropriateness of this was realised and the whole machinery of education and propaganda was mobilised to produce a new and more attractive image of the peasant and his role in a transformed rural environment. By this time, however, millions had enjoyed for themselves the working and recreational amenities of urban life and even if their migration could not be judged successful by strict economic criteria, many perhaps retained hope of improvement and indulged in self-deceptions of a type impossible to those subjected to the harsh facts of village life, but which once experienced in the city are not easily foregone.

The mechanics of migration

The mechanisms by which immigration took place were quite complex. The first point to establish is that the legal rights of migrants were for most of our period ambiguous. On the one hand

---

[1] In 1955, incomes in Shanghai's agricultural suburbs reportedly rose 56% on the 1954 levels. At the same time large cash and grain incomes were promised for the post-collectivisation period. 'Agricultural Cooperatives in the city's suburbs completely demonstrate their superiority', *HWJP* 17 Jan. 1957. The key role of food availability in the rural areas is described in 'In P'eng Lai District more than 400 unemployed [workers] have returned to rural production', *HWJP* 10 Aug. 1955.

there was a clear statement in the Constitution of 1954 that citizens had the right to choose their place of residence and work. This might be called the higher law. Below this, however, residence and employment were subject to a mass of specific directives and regulations aimed at preventing migration. This conflict was never properly resolved, although on many occasions frustrated migrants appealed against the administrative rules to the higher law of the Constitution in which they claimed their freedom of movement was guaranteed.[1] The answer to such appeals was usually in terms of the necessity of constricting lesser freedoms in order to protect the higher freedoms of full employment, etc.

The administrative rules by which the Government tried to stop urban immigration fell into three main categories. First, there were the population registration regulations, which required the population to carry a form of identity card which had to be checked and approved as part of the procedure for legitimate movement. Second, there were the regulations governing changes in employment. And third, by the mid-1950s there were regulations governing the control of primary foodstuffs in the urban areas which were also an explicit part of the population control apparatus.

None of these controls could be said to have been fully effective prior to 1958. The registration regulations failed because prior to 1956 rural cadres were frequently glad to be rid of surplus labour and were therefore willing to facilitate migration by giving migrants proper papers. When the migrant arrived in the city, with or without papers, a variety of alternatives were open to him. If he had no papers there was a black market in them. Alternatively, an employer or illicit labour broker who was anxious for labour would either ignore the irregularity or possibly indulge in falsification himself.[2] Failing these possibilities, a migrant might remain without papers by working for an illicit firm or by working on his own account in small scale production or services. In the last resort, our migrant

---

[1] 'Is it contrary to the Constitution to refuse permission to the rural population to come and take up residence in the towns?' *NFJP* 28 Oct. 1957, and, 'Is this lack of freedom of residence?' *Kung jen jih pao* (Workers daily, hereafter *KJJP*) 26 Sep. 1957.
[2] 'Check up and deal with units and personnel who privately [illicitly], hire temporary workers', *Ch'ing tao jih pao* (Tsingtao daily) 6 Dec. 1957. See also an experience described in Suzanne Labin, *La condition humaine en Chine communiste* (1959), chapter 12.

might simply remain unemployed and live with relatives. Family and kinship relationships remained important in the 1950s and there is evidence that this was a crucial factor in enabling migrants to evade migration controls.[1]

The relationship between population registration and employment was a close one and the implication of what we have said above is that there were in urban areas throughout the 1950s what may be termed free and black labour markets. By free, we mean that employers had the right to hire without reference to the Labour Bureau. By black, we mean that even when there was no such right, employers were able to circumvent the official hiring procedures. The motive for such hiring was that illicitly hired labour was often cheaper (in that such labour involved no welfare payments and possibly lower than official wages) and also more easily dispensed with than labour acquired through the offices of the Labour Bureaux.[2] Obviously illicit hiring was particularly easy for illicit firms and the problem did not arise in the case of illicit self-employment – which many migrants resorted to. The evidence for labour markets of this kind is abundant and is discussed more fully later.[3]

Finally we have to ask why food control was such an ineffective instrument of population control. Food control was not introduced until late 1953, and is not therefore relevant to the migration before that date. After this migrants were either able to obtain official grain as a result of lax and liberal grain administration or they circumvented food control by recourse to free and black markets.[4] The free markets consisted of (a) the markets in secondary foodstuffs, and (b) food sold in restaurants and canteens where ration coupons were not usually required.[5] The black market consisted of foodstuffs

[1] Surveys of migrants in Harbin, Tientsin and Shanghai all showed that *the majority* of migrants were staying in cities with relatives – many of whom were cadres. 'Those who have come from the country should go back', *JMJP* 22 May 1957; 'Tens of thousands of peasants infiltrate the city', *TKP* (Peking) 3 Jun. 1957; 'Stop outsiders infiltrating into Shanghai', *WHP* 21 Dec. 1957.

[2] *JMJP* 19 Aug. 1957.   [3] See Chapter 4.

[4] 'Stop completely the practice of giving grain ration cards to members of the rural population who have infiltrated into the towns and cities', *Shan hsi jih pao* (Shansi daily) 28 Jul. 1957.

[5] In Changchun, for example, 12% of the city grain supply went through restaurants and canteens and attempts to control this met with resistance. 'Readjust the work of planned grain supply as quickly as possible', *Ch'ang ch'un jih pao* (Changchun daily) 11 Jan. 1957.

illicitly marketed by the peasants or by workers and staff with rations sufficiently liberal to give them a marketable surplus.[1]

Our conclusion is, therefore, that up to 1958 immigration was facilitated by liberal grain administration and a group of licit and illicit free markets in food and employment which reinforced each other in ways that enabled migrants to evade every aspect of the Government's machinery for population control.

Most emigration in our period was the result of official pressure and the emigration mechanism was therefore altogether less complex – particularly if the object of emigration was an illicit migrant. In these cases, emigration was normally effected by a combination of rigorous police check ups; 'campaigns' and propaganda; the provision of transport or fares; and liaison work with rural authorities to ensure that migrants were warmly received on return. The problem of reintegrating migrants into the rural community was a very serious one. In the early 1950s migrants were often given a little working capital in cash and kind but this usually proved an inadequate base from which to establish economic viability; taking these experiences into account, we are convinced that the problems of rural repatriation were an important factor in explaining the character of Higher Level Agricultural Cooperatives established in 1956. For by comparison with the Lower Cooperatives the regulations for these were clearly designed to facilitate the return to the countryside of poor and landless peasants and others whom the authorities were anxious to clear out from the cities.[2] It was no accident that the High Tide of Socialism followed shortly after a massive *hsia fang* movement.

The problem of moving bona fide and long term residents out of the cities was more difficult since it called for a persuasive rather than coercive approach. But persuasion was rarely successful on its

[1] 'The people of the city voluntarily reduce their grain rations by more than 30,000 *chin*', *STJP* 13 Jan. 1957.

[2] The regulations for both Higher and Lower stage cooperatives stipulated that ex-servicemen, handicraftsmen etc. should be admitted. The elimination of rent payment, however, was the key to making this a workable proposition. The Lower stage regulations are in *Chung Hua jen min kung ho kuo fa kuei hui pien* (Compendium of laws and regulations of the Chinese People's Republic) 1955 No. 2, July–December (1956), pp. 624–59. The Higher stage regulations are in the same series, 1956 No. 3, January–June, pp. 292–314.

own and the Government had to rely heavily on campaigns for urban emigration conducted at times when the political temperature was high, and when people therefore were reluctant to lay themselves open to charges of political deviation. Thus the most successful *hsia fang* in Shanghai (that of 1955) followed the spring purges of the Shanghai Party and bureaucracy, and we find that the national *hsia fang* campaign of 1957 was closely related to the virulent anti-rightest campaign of the same year.[1]

Conclusions

Our main conclusion is that immigration to the cities intensified unemployment and was also a cause of over-manning, or what has been aptly named 'supply-induced' employment.[2] The magnitude of the effect on open unemployment is indicated by the Shanghai data where we showed that the net migrant addition to the supply of job seekers was 17%. If we assume for a moment that the labour supply was homogenous, the implication is that immigration almost doubled the level of unemployment.

[1] Franz Shurmann, *Ideology and organization in Communist China* (1966), pp. 333–4; *KSJP* 8 Dec. 1957.
[2] D.C. Mead, chapter 6.

4

EMPLOYMENT FLUCTUATIONS
AND THEIR CONSEQUENCES

In the last chapter we were interested in the determinants of employment trends over the whole period from 1949 to 1957. Now we wish to consider the nature and importance of urban employment fluctuations.

In our first chapter we presented some analysis of the major indicators of urban economic fluctuations and the data showed that output fluctuations were associated with employment change. We also argued that violent employment change was associated with loss of control over the labour market. At that point we emphasised the problem of employment control at the peaks of activity and this was indeed the most serious problem. In this chapter however we shall show that control in the troughs was not easy either, and in our conclusion we argue that the consequences of the overall failure to control urban hiring were aggravation of structural unemployment and of the phenomenon of overmanning.

Let us briefly look at the data on employment fluctuations again. At the national level we have no index of fluctuations of the total urban labour force but we do have data on changes in industry and construction and these are included in Table 31 together with some local data.

These data show that industrial employment was fairly volatile at the national level while employment in construction fluctuated violently. At the local level we have data for Tientsin and Shenyang which are interesting since they show that employment fluctuations were similar in pattern in both key-point and non-key-point cities.

All these series tend to confirm our view that the peak years of urban economic activity were 1951, 1953 and 1956; and the data for many individual cities suggest that 1956 was a year of altogether extraordinary employment absorption.[1]

[1] Emerson's non-agricultural employment series does not exactly confirm our view of

Apart from these series we have other quantitative and qualitative information that confirm labour shortages in 1951, 1953 and 1956.

Table 31. *Employment fluctuations: national and local data, 1949–57*

National	(% change in total employment compared with previous years)							
	1950	1951	1952	1953	1954	1955	1956	1957
Industry[a]	+11	+29	+20	+16	+ 4	− 4	+22	+ 6
Construction[b]	+100	+50	+75	+107	− 3	− 8	+53	−35

Local	(% change in the number of persons placed in jobs compared with the previous year)							
	1950	1951	1952	1953	1954	1955	1956	1957
Shanghai[c]	−49	+75	−57	+120	−92	–	–	−53
Tientsin[d]	–	+233	−10	0	−44	− 5	+210	–
Shenyang[e]	–	–	+21	+32	−45	0	+233	–

NOTE: While the national data show net changes in employment resulting from job placements, and employment losses through retirement, unemployment, etc., the local data are for job placements only. Close comparison of national and local data is therefore not possible.

SOURCES:
[a] Table 8, Chapter 1.
[b] Table 9, Chapter 1.
[c] *CFJP* 23 Sep. 1952; *JMJP* 13 Sep. 1952; *CFJP* 19 Jan. 1951; *WHP* 28 Jun. 1954; *HHPYK* 1954 No. 5, pp. 157–8; *CFJP* 9 Jan. 1955; *HWJP* 28 Aug. 1957; Chapter 2, p. 39.
[d] 'Who says that unemployment has increased?' *LT* 1957 No. 15, p. 19.
[e] 'The unemployment increase in 1956 is twelve times that of 1955', *Shen yang jih pao* (Shenyang daily, hereafter *SYJP*) 2 Aug. 1957.

In 1951, skilled and experienced labour was in particularly short supply in all cities and Shanghai reports indicate that shortages extended well down the skill scale and that the Labour Bureau was

the peak years. In particular, the estimate of a 1% increase in employment in 1956 bears little relation to the detailed picture of employment change in that year which can be constructed from the local data. The key to explaining the differences between non-agricultural employment and urban employment in 1956 is the performance of the traditional non-agricultural sectors after the rural and urban collectivisations. In the rural areas, collectivisation led to curtailment of handicraft activity, while in the urban areas the demand for consumer goods, generated by high overall levels of activity and the wage reform, allowed the traditional sector to expand. 'Why has output of locally produced paper declined?' *JMJP* 11 Nov. 1956; 'Increase and utilise the output of locally produced iron', *TKP* (Peking) 31 Dec. 1956; 'Some problems hindering the development of rural handicrafts', *Ch'ing hai jih pao* (Tsinghai daily, hereafter *CHJP*) 17 Jan. 1957.

unable to satisfy employers' demands for labour of all types.[1] Further indications of the tightening labour situation consist of reports of the lengthening of working hours and increasing work intensity.[2] In 1953, employment increased sharply again and there are numerous reports of labour shortages, particularly in the construction sector.[3] For 1956, evidence of labour market tensions is overwhelming. Shanghai, Harbin, Paotou, Ching Te Chen, Lanchow, Swatow, Chan Chiang and the provinces of Heilungkiang, Shantung and Chekiang all reported that they experienced 'full employment' in that year.[4] Our information on Shanghai confirms that demand for labour in 1956 encompassed the entire skill range and all the main industrial and transport sectors. At the national level we also know that there was an acute shortage of graduates, since 70% of departmental requests for graduates could not be met.[5]

The evidence suggests that throughout the 1950s these fluctuations were an important factor in undermining the formal hiring mechanism and in making effective employment control impossible –

[1] 'In the last two years [The Labour Bureau] has helped 20,000 workers and staff to find employment', CFJP 8 Nov. 1951; '100,000 unemployed find work', CFJP 8 Jan. 1952.

[2] 'Private clothing factories in Wuhan violate labour policy and neglect workers' health', CCJP 14 Nov. 1951 (SCMP 228). This article reported that days of 14–18 hours were being worked and that sickness rates, etc., were increasing.

[3] For examples of acute shortages of skilled and construction labour in Shanghai, Anshan and Shenyang see, Tung pei jih pao (North East daily, hereafter TPJP) 15 Mar. 1953; LT 1953 No. 10.

[4] CFJP 18 Aug. 1956; Ha erh pin jih pao (Harbin daily) 25 Oct. 1956. NMKJP 26 Oct. 1956 (SCMP 1434); 'The unemployment phenomenon has been basically eliminated in Ching Te Chen', Chiang hsi jih pao (Kiangsi daily) 31 Dec. 1956; 'Lanchow has basically eliminated unemployment,' Chung kuo ch'ing nien pao (China Youth daily, hereafter CKCNP) 2 Aug. 1956; 'The unemployment phenomenon in Nan P'ing has been basically eliminated', FCJP 9 Aug. 1956; 'The unemployed of Swatow are now all in employment', NFJP 4 Sep. 1956; 'All the unemployed in Chan Chiang are now in employment', NFJP 20 Jul. 1956; 'Actively solve and correctly understand some remaining workers livelihood problems', HLCJP 15 Nov. 1956; 'The unemployed in Shantung all get employment', KJJP 13 Sep. 1956; 'No unemployment in Chekiang', NCNA 27 Jul. 1956 (SCMP 1341).

[5] Labour shortages were reported in the heavy, textile, construction and transport industries. 'Report on the implementation of the National Five Year Plan in Shanghai', CFJP 11 Aug. 1956; 'Some views on local heavy industry work', CFJP 12 Aug. 1956; 'Some views on local heavy industry work', BFJP 12 Aug. 1956; 'Develop the potential of Shanghai's textile industry', CFJP 13 Aug. 1956. There was also a national shortage of High-School graduates. Only 30% of requests by departments for graduates could be met in 1956; 'Contradiction in the supply and demand for university graduates', CFJP 2 Jun. 1957.

although we must qualify this by pointing out that official procedures were themselves in a state of flux, so that what was violated was not so much a static set of rules, as the Labour Ministry's ideal of a labour market in which all hiring was either arranged through the Bureaux or subject to their approval.[1]

Before 1958 this ideal proved unrealisable since throughout the whole period hiring continued through the licit and illicit markets which were described briefly in the last chapter.[2] The relative importance of these markets and the official mechanisms is difficult to judge. But we do have one report that claims that of the additional 16,000,000 persons who entered non-agricultural employment between 1949 and 1957, only 4,000,000 went directly through the Labour Bureaux.[3] The share of the licit and illicit markets in the remainder is unknown although we know that the black markets were particularly important in the private, construction and traditional sector.[4]

The links between employment fluctuations and the inability of the Labour Bureaux to control hiring were numerous. Let us look at the peaks of activity first. In these, the Bureaux were incapable of handling the rapid growth in the demand for labour because of lack of personnel and the rigidities of the official job placement processes. The personnel problem, both in the Bureaux and in the labour departments of economic enterprises and other organisations, was a shortage of both quality and quantity.[5] Reports of the lack of personnel for labour work are very common in the 1950s, and after the fiasco of 1956, when a planned increase of workers and staff of 840,000 resulted in an actual increase of 2,300,000, it was revealed that in many areas and organisations machinery for labour adminis-

---

[1] The evolution of the official hiring mechanism is described in Chapters 5 to 8.

[2] The status of the hired and hirer is crucial to the distinction between free and black hiring. Black-market hiring involved either an illicit enterprise or an employee who had left his previous employment without permission or who was an illegal migrant. On occasions illegal hirers were severely punished in the Courts, see for example, 'Illegal capitalists Yin Chih-hsien and Ku Wei-jen are given prison sentences', *CFJP* 24 Nov. 1954.

[3] 'The way to employment is broad', *JMJP* 19 Aug. 1957; *WHP* 14 Jun. 1959.

[4] 'An illegal capitalist severely contravenes labour policy', *LT* 1955 No. 10, p. 31 (among other crimes this man gave peasants false documents); 'Implement the labour employment policy of combining official placing with finding jobs by one's own efforts', *CFJP* 28 Jun. 1954 (*SCMP* 984).

[5] 'Don't make us like ballbearings', *LT* 1956 No. 10, p. 23; see also Chapter 5.

tration had never been set up.[1] Thus, even in Shanghai, where one would expect relative maturity of labour administration, we estimate that in 1957 at least 40% of the labour force fell within neither the local labour plan or the plan of a centrally controlled ministry.[2]

Complexity and rigidity of formal rules characterised most aspects of the Labour Bureaux work and the procedures for hiring and job placement exemplify this. Up to 1957, an enterprise request for labour involved at least four other organisations: the Municipal Bureau, the District Labour Office, the Street Labour Office, and the Street Residents Committee. Thus it is not surprising that in one town it was reported that to obtain labour through official channels took up to eight days. In addition, the Labour Bureaux made a hiring charge which enterprises resented and could avoid paying if they resorted to unofficial labour markets.[3]

Given these weaknesses, it is not surprising that when the economy was expanding rapidly the Bureaux were unable to satisfy the demand for labour and that as alternative employment opportunities opened in every direction, control of even limited sectors of the labour market became impossible.[4] The result was that illicit hiring accelerated and that in 1956, under overwhelming pressure, the Bureaux accepted the situation and allowed workers and hirers to act freely in the labour market.[5]

Another factor which contributed to the breakdown of employment administration in the booms was the high level of demand for

[1] 'A summary of the experience of 1956; reform labour and wage work', *CHCC* 1957 No. 8, pp. 9–13.

[2] *HWJP* 28 Aug. 1957; *HHPYK* 1957 No. 2, pp. 87–9.

[3] 'The Labour Bureau in Chengchow municipality smashes conservative thinking and old regulations', *LT* 1958 No. 10, p. 35.

[4] 'Recruitment of workers and job jumping are serious problems in Shanghai', *CFJP* 11 Oct. 1951 (*SCMP* 212); 'The phenomenon of wild hiring and the blind enlargement of the labour force is developing', *CFJP* 24 Jan. 1953; an interesting survey of the origins of the labour force in a sample of illicit enterprises in 1957 is, 'See the problems of individual handicraft development from [the experience of] a few cities', *TKP* (Peking) 16 Feb. 1956. This showed that 18·4% of the labour force were peasants; 39% were women and others of no previous occupation; 25% were persons left unemployed after the socialisation of commerce and industry; 15% were unemployed workers; other minor categories accounted for the remainder.

[5] A most spectacular example of free and black hiring in 1956 is the experience of Szechuan Province, where in six months 311,142 persons were illicitly hired; 'The phenomenon of private hiring and snatching in Szechuan is very serious', *LT* 1956 No. 12, p. 27. The relaxation of control in Shanghai was announced by the head of the Labour Bureau, *CFJP* 18 Aug. 1956.

consumption goods which made entry into small scale production and commerce easy and profitable.

The third link between upswings and employment control was the behaviour of wages. Upswings tended to be associated with some loss of control over wages and this meant that unplanned wage movements often provided further incentive for workers to evade official employment procedures. This loss of control over wages was partly related to the cyclical upswings in the private and traditional sectors, since these upswings were accompanied by rising wages and incomes which attracted workers and staff from the public sector and peasants from the rural areas. But in the public sector also, violation of wage plans was common in the upswings, due both to the failure of the Labour Bureaux to meet the requirements of enterprises and to the general shift of emphasis from cost to physical output targets.[1]

Failure to control hiring was not confined to the upswings, for it was noticeable also in the slack years of 1954–55 and 1957. The scale of the black market in 1955 is indicated in an article which described the activities of a labour broker who hired 3,200 workers to go to Wuhan, drawing on such diverse areas as Shanghai, Honan, Hunan and Szechuan.[2] Brokers and enterprises were again reported to be very active in 1957. For example, 17,000 peasants were illicitly hired by brokers from sixteen counties in Anhui *after* the publication of the new ruling prohibiting such activities.[3] While in Tsinan city there was a regular labour market at 6 a.m. every morning on the outskirts of the city, where to the irritation of the urban unemployed, enterprises recruited up to 300 peasants a day.[4]

The evident ability of illegal labour brokers and unscrupulous enterprises to operate on a big scale in these years is explained by the fact that they were dealing in a buyers' market. Lack of employment

[1] 'Recruitment of workers and job jumping are serious problems in Shanghai', *CFJP* 11 Oct. 1951; 'Wage adjustment work already set up', *Canton kung shang jih pao* (The weekly magazine of Canton private industry and commerce) 1954 No. 34; 'Resolutely smash the wild attacks of capitalists', *CKCNP* 21 Aug. 1957.

[2] 'Correct the phenomenon of chaotic hiring of personnel', *LT* 1955 No. 12, p. 32.

[3] 'Take severe measures to prevent private hiring of temporary workers', *An hui jih pao* (Anhwei daily) 18 Dec. 1957.

[4] 'The free market in labour must be eliminated', *Chi nan jih pao* (Tsinan daily) 9 Jan. 1958.

absorption in the slack years must have made workers prefer risks and lower wages in the illicit market to remaining unemployed.

In addition to illicit markets, the years of slow growth also forced the Labour Bureaux to relax formal hiring rules. For when economic activity was depressed, the Bureaux found themselves with administrative responsibility for an unemployment problem which they were fundamentally incapable of alleviating. No possible change in labour administration could affect the demand for labour and the Bureaux machinery for settling the unemployed was not effective in periods when work was scarce. The Bureaux reaction was therefore to retain, and indeed tighten, control over key sectors of the labour force such as the skilled and construction workers, while at the same time tolerating a substantial degree of freedom in other sectors of the labour market. In other words the Bureaux encouraged the expansion of licit free markets in labour.[1]

To summarise, our argument is that fluctuations in the urban economy were a crucial factor in the inability of the Labour Bureaux to maintain control, or even keep informed of, hiring in the labour market. For neither at the peaks or troughs could the Bureaux perform their functions effectively. At the peaks they could not satisfy demand for labour rapidly enough, and in the troughs they did not constitute an efficient mechanism for distributing unemployed job seekers among such opportunities as were available.

Violent fluctuations of employment and the failure of the Labour Bureaux to control hiring had serious consequences both for overmanning and structural unemployment. During periods of economic upsurge, the labour force expanded to a size greater than could be justified by the short-term growth prospects of the urban economy; so that when the growth rate subsided, a high proportion of the additional workers and staff were found to be unnecessary. This problem was aggravated by the extraordinary speed of the upsurges because this led to the phenomenon of quantity/quality substitution in the labour force. When labour requirements increased rapidly, employers responded by substituting large numbers of less skilled

---

[1] It should be noted that official toleration of free labour markets did not legalise black ones. Even the most liberal relaxation of free markets rarely allowed the hiring of peasants.

workers and staff for the smaller numbers of skilled or experienced staff actually needed. The evidence for this sort of process at all skill levels of workers and staff is substantial.[1] But of course, within quite short periods of time the skill level of the new recruits rose, which combined with the slackening of the urban economic growth rate led to redundancy. Had the excessive intakes of labour in 1951, 1953 and 1956 been easily reversible the problem would not have been so serious, but they were not. It is true that some temporary staff could be dispensed with, some new female entrants to the labour force could be persuaded to return to domestic work, and migrants in illicit employment could be rounded up and returned to the countryside. But outside of these groups there were large numbers taken on as permanent employees – or converted from temporary to permanent status during the upswing – who could not be removed by the normal processes of labour administration.

In this situation persuasive techniques could be resorted to, but pressures to reduce employment were resisted, not only by workers themselves, but by managements of economic enterprises and bureaucratic organisations who were anxious to hold reserves of labour against the day when the authorities might again place enormous and sudden demands upon them, and who were in any case predictably averse to reduction in the size of their organisations, since such reduction would be reflected in reduction of their power and prestige.[2] Moreover even when, as in 1955, the leadership of the bureaucratic and industrial systems were forced to initiate man-power reduction policies, the power leakages in the multi-level systems that they were responsible for were so great that basic level labour management cadres remained *more* responsive to pressures for an expansion of supply induced employment from below, than to the demands for manpower economies from above.

[1] 'Some views on solving the problem of skilled labour shortage', *LT* 1954 No. 11, p. 19; 'Report on the Shanghai budget out-turns for 1956 and the draft estimates for 1957', *HWJP* 28 Aug. 1957. The quantity/quality mechanism was equally important at the administrative level. As some cadres put it, 'the skill level of our cadres is very low, therefore it is always good to have large numbers of them'; 'Conscientiously do the work of reorganisation and the setting up of a simplified administrative structure', *CFJP* 18 Apr. 1955.

[2] For example, in mid-1955 Shanghai managers resisted the transference of workers to other cities; 'Send even more workers to participate in key-point construction on a basis of rotation', *JMJP* 4 May 1955.

In sum then, the combination of extreme variations in the demand for labour, the quantity/quality substitution phenomenon, and the irreversibility of hiring, combined to make periodic crises of over-manning unavoidable. These crises were all the more serious because economic enterprises and bureaucratic organisations were capable of putting up tremendous resistance to pressures on them to reduce their size – resistance which could only be overcome by a full-scale, coercive mobilisation of political power.

Fluctuations were also directly related to the growth of unemployment, since the upswings gave urban employment opportunities for the rural work force which led to unplanned migration. The upswing of 1953, for example, led directly to an acceleration of rural–urban migration and in 1956 the city authorities were themselves urgently recruiting temporary labour in the rural areas. When the booms subsided many of these workers found themselves unemployed, but were reluctant to return to the rural areas. They therefore lingered on in the city as unproductive additions to urban costs.

This analysis has general applicability, but in conclusion it is worth noting the special importance of the construction industry in these processes, since as we shall see later, attempts to control the labour force of this industry were to have far reaching consequences for all labour planning.

The construction labour force was reported to have grown from 200,000 in 1949 to 1,900,000 in 1957; its average size in these years was 1,479,000 and it reached a peak in 1956, when the force totalled 2,951,000.[1] This does not represent a large construction force for a country the size of China undergoing rapid growth, and in absolute terms it is not much larger than the force of 1,000,000 full time construction workers estimated to have been working in China in the nineteenth century.[2] However, the combination of a growth rate of nearly 30% per annum and violent fluctuations as shown in Table 31, meant that the problems of labour management outlined

[1] The measurement of the construction labour force presents very difficult problems. See Emerson (1965), pp. 149–50.

[2] Chang Chung-li, *The income of the Chinese gentry* (1962), 314 n. The rapid growth of the construction labour force in China paralleled that of the USSR during its First Plan. However, the size of the Chinese force, relative to total population, was considerably smaller. Soviet data for 1929, 1932 and 1937 appear in Harry Schwartz, *Russia's Soviet economy* (1958), p. 521.

in this chapter were found in intensified form in the construction sector. And it must be remembered that the fluctuations in our table are annual, and that these were compounded by seasonal variations in the demand for construction labour.

As a result of this, we find that there was an acute contradiction in construction labour management arising from the conflict between short-run cost objectives on the one hand, and employment and population control objectives on the other. For the pressures to minimise costs caused enterprises to respond to fluctuations by maintaining a high labour turnover and by having a high proportion of temporary workers in their work gangs. Thus the ideal construction worker was a peasant with seasonal availability and secondary sources of income (from agriculture).[1] The effect of this was to make the construction industry a major channel for illicit migrants to enter the urban labour force and also to inhibit the growth of a stable, skilled labour force of the type that was wanted in the long run.[2] This conflict had important implications for the whole field of labour control and in later chapters we shall trace its handling and resolution.

[1] In Changchun, for example, 70% of the basic construction labour force were temporaries; 30% of these also worked in agriculture and a further 30% had other sources of income, *Ch'ang ch'un jih pao* (Changchun daily) 23 Oct. 1957. In Hangchow in 1955, 70% of the construction force was reported to own land, 'Important work in labour assignment', *LT* 1955 No. 8, pp. 4-5.

[2] A survey in Tientsin, for example, showed that nearly half of the temporary construction work force were illicit migrants. *LT* 1955 No. 8, pp. 2-4.

PART TWO

EMPLOYMENT POLICY
AND
ADMINISTRATION

5

THE FOUNDATION OF THE LABOUR BUREAUX AND THE BEGINNINGS OF EMPLOYMENT ADMINISTRATION, 1949–52

INTRODUCTION

In this and the following two chapters, we shall analyse the development of employment policy and administration between 1949 and 1957. Our framework is historical, since no other approach enables us to analyse the sequence of interaction between the basic problems of urban labour absorption and control and the policies and institutions designed to solve them. These interactions were complex, and in following them through one realises that not only is it difficult to describe definitively the regulations and practices governing the labour markets at any one time, but from what we do know, it is clear that Chinese labour laws and practices did not constitute a stable and geographically uniform system. For as we shall see, the search for solutions to basic problems led to continuous policy and institutional modifications which themselves created new problems and initiated further change. The limit to the feasible variations in most of the rules governing labour market administration explains why the process of institutional evolution which we shall be examining appears to have some cyclical characteristics.

Our analysis is concerned with employment work at two levels. The first is that of overall policy making and the second, that of labour administration at the local level. The latter is largely the work of the Labour Bureaux, but also includes the work of other departments concerned with economic administration and population control. The background to overall employment policy was analysed in Chapter 1 and the specific context of labour administration – structural unemployment and violent fluctuation – was analysed in Chapters 3 and 4.

87

It is hoped that although our method is historical, our results will be of more than historical interest. For what we are analysing is the way in which pursuit of basic economic objectives led the Chinese from tolerance of a virtually free labour market, through a series of experiments, to the establishment of a group of institutions designed to give the state complete and direct control over population movement and employment decisions. When one considers the scale of China's urban labour market, the paucity of the resources available to administer it, and the precedent of Russian failures in labour control, the bid to achieve total control seems extraordinarily ambitious. In these chapters we shall try and explain why it was that by the end of 1957, there seemed to be no alternative to this that was both economically reasonable and politically acceptable.

1949–52: POLICY: THE UNDERLYING VISION

On 24 April 1945, Mao Tse-tung addressed the Seventh Party Congress on the question of 'Coalition Government'. This was a crucial moment for the Party which was then exploring the possibility of post-war collaboration with the Kuomintang, and in his opening address, Mao spelt out his ideas for the development of China after the conclusion of the war. The speech is unusual in Chinese communist literature in that it is focused neither on immediate issues nor on the eschatology of a remote future. Power was approaching and what was needed was a working view of the medium term. This Mao provided. We are concerned here with one small section of the speech, that dealing with the agrarian question. In this section Mao said, 'The peasants are the future industrial workers of China and tens of millions of them will go into the cities. For if China wants to construct large scale, indigenous industry and to build a great number of large, modern cities: then she will have to undergo a long process of transformation in which the rural population become residents of the cities.' There is much in this speech which might be interpreted as tactical, but one can see no reason for thinking that this applies to the sentence quoted above. On the contrary, it seems to us to express Mao's genuine conviction and to be the key to an understanding of employment policy in the early 1950s. And it was this expectation, that industrial growth and the development of socialist institutions would combine to eliminate unemployment and secure continuous rural–urban labour transfer, that underlay employment policy up to mid-1955.[1]

THE ESTABLISHMENT OF THE LABOUR BUREAUX

The establishment of the Labour Bureaux at the provincial and municipal levels was formally accomplished in May 1950; although we know that in Shanghai, at least, prior to that date, labour administration had been the responsibility of the old Kuomintang Labour Office. Thus the Labour Bureaux appear to be an important example of an urban organisation which preserved direct continuity with the pre-revolutionary era, and as we shall see later, this continuity extended to the details of policy and administrative practice.[2]

The 1950 directives stated that the Bureaux were to be under the direct leadership of provincial and municipal governments and that their basic duty was to implement decisions and directives originating at the local level or from the central Ministry of Labour. More specifically, the Bureaux' duties were as follows: (*a*) to supervise (*chien tu*) the implementation of labour laws in both public and private sectors; (*b*) to mediate or formally arbitrate disputes between Labour and Capital in the private sector and between management and workers in the public sector; (*c*) to examine, approve and register collective contracts governing wages and conditions in the private sector; (*d*) to supervise the implementation of unified wage standards; (*e*) to supervise and guide insurance work; (*f*) to inspect (*chien ch'a*) health and safety work – especially for women and children; (*g*) to supervise and lead the organisation of labour

[1] Mao Tse-tung, *Hsüan chi* (Collected Works), (1964), p. 1079. A similar view is expressed in 'How should the urban economy be managed?' *CCCP* Ser. 8, No. 14, pp. 179–81.

[2] The directives and a speech about them by Li Li-san are in *Hua Tung ch'ü ts'ai cheng ching chi fa ling hui pien* (1951), Vol. 2, pp. 1678–89. Another relevant directive is in *Chung yang lao tung fa ling hui pien* (Compendium of Central Government labour laws), (1953), p. 33. Li Li-san was the author of the famous 'Li Li-san line', and was removed from the Party leadership in 1930. He was Minister of Labour until 1954 when Ma Wen-jui took over. Ma disappeared in the Cultural Revolution. It is an important reflection on the status of labour work that both ministers have been politically insignificant.

discipline, premium and model worker activities; (*h*) to cooperate with educational and Union authorities in establishing spare-time education facilities for workers; (*i*) to investigate and register unemployed persons, regulate manpower usage and settle the unemployed.

The organisational counterpart to these duties at the municipal level consisted of two divisions (*shih*), one for general administration and one for statistical work; and five sections (*k'o*), one each for labour relations, inspection and supervision, wages, insurance and safety. In addition, the Bureaux were to establish an office (*so*) for introducing the unemployed to work and organise committees for arbitration, manpower regulation and safety. Below the municipal level, the Bureaux could set up further divisions, sections and offices according to local needs.

From this official account of the tasks and organisation of the Bureaux we can draw a number of conclusions. First, the range of duties entrusted to the Bureaux was considerable and this implied either a large number of cadres or the ability to adopt a highly flexible policy of switching from one task to another as the current requirements of labour policy dictated. Little is known about the numbers employed in labour administration, but the fragments of evidence that we have suggest that they were inadequate in relation to the range of the Bureaux tasks and the number of enterprises and units for which they were responsible. Certainly there was no special training school for labour administrators before 1956.[1]

This chronic under-staffing was a major factor limiting the ability of the Bureaux to handle the full range of their duties simultaneously, and it also explains the necessity for frequent shifts of emphasis in

[1] In Peking, in 1957, the *municipal* Labour Bureau employed a staff of 121 persons; while in Shanghai the *district* level organisation of Kiang Ning was reported as having a staff of 36. This would indicate that in the late 1950s the Bureau organisation in Shanghai must have comprised about 1,000 persons. This figure should be related to labour administration in about 17,000 productive enterprises, 30,000 to 40,000 commercial units and an unknown number of bureaucratic organisations. 'Peking Municipality Labour Bureau's simplification and *hsia fang* work', *LT* 1958 No. 1, p. 13; 'Personnel diminished; productivity increased', *LT* 1958 No. 9, p. 30; 'Go to the small factory', *CFJP* 12 Apr. 1957; *Szu ying shang yeh ti she hui chu i kai tsao* (*tzu liao*) (1963), p. 140. The Peking Labour Cadre School was established in 1956 and in its first two years trained 480 cadres of whom 299 were specialists in wages and safety work. *LT* 1958 No. 6, p. 4.

Bureaux effort and the necessity of periodic mobilisation of other organisations to do labour work whenever a task of real urgency occurred.

A second point to notice in the directives is that they reflect the official view that the Bureaux' work was primarily connected with workers' welfare, rather than with direct employment and wage planning. Manpower control for example, although mentioned, does not even rate a section of its own, and in the list of Bureaux tasks is squeezed uncomfortably between two aspects of unemployment administration.[1]

Finally, a fundamental weakness of the directives was that they specified a broad range of tasks for the Bureaux, performance of which required direct involvement in the labour administration of economic and bureaucratic organisations as well as coordination with other Government organs. Yet nowhere did the directive give a satisfactory account of Bureaux authority or detailed guidance for the resolution of conflicts which the Bureaux work was bound to generate. In theory the Bureaux were given power to inspect labour administration, obtain statistics, and make 'proposals'. 'Proposals' were to be treated with 'serious consideration' by managements and 'where possible' implemented. There was however no obligation on managements to act on Bureaux suggestions and in the event of outright refusal to cooperate, the directive stated simply that the Bureaux could take the matter to higher (unspecified) levels.

This lack of clearly defined authority was to be very important in our period and together with the lack of administrative resources was a major explanation of the Bureaux ineffectiveness.

In addition to the formal directives, our knowledge of the origins of the Labour Bureaux is supplemented by a speech by Li Li-san, Minister of Labour, which is valuable in that it confirms that official thinking in 1950 conformed closely to our interpretation of the formal directives. In his speech, Li Li-san made it clear that the Bureaux were to concentrate on welfare issues. He argued that the transformation of the economic status of Chinese workers would take a long time and that it would be the duty of the Labour Bureaux

---

[1] In Manchuria the Bureaux were in fact already engaged in manpower planning of a crude kind. The plans for 1950 and 1951 are in *LT* 1951 No. 6.

to supervise the details of this gradual process. In particular the Bureaux had to watch capitalists and their managers to ensure that the limits of exploitation were carefully controlled – exploitation still being technically tolerated in the theory and practice of New Democracy.

Li Li-san also emphasised the work of mediation. The background to this was that in the period immediately after 1949 labour discipline had dissolved in a frenzy of anarchic behaviour. This had had serious consequences for both output and price stability. Li Li-san stated that the Bureaux' function was to mediate in conflicts in the private sector, which in the context of the time implied that the Bureaux were to come to the defence of the capitalists.[1]

Mediation, however, was not to be confined to the private sector. In the public sector the Bureaux were to mediate between workers and managements and in practice, the role assigned to the Bureaux was almost exactly the same as that assigned to the Trades Unions by Lenin; they were to be a bulwark against the inroads of an inefficient and unjust bureaucracy.

The immediate problems

The most pressing task facing the Bureaux on their formation was unemployment. In early 1950, unemployment rose sharply under the impact of drastic budgetary measures designed to control the current inflation. These measures included a programme of manpower reduction in the public sector and in Government organs which added to the unemployment effects of the squeeze in the private sector.[2] The seriousness of the problem was recognised in speeches by Mao Tse-tung, Chou En-lai and Ch'en Yün. In Shanghai where the situation was aggravated by renewed military hostilities, the labour situation was described as tense and the Mayor, Ch'en Yi,

[1] Mediation work had previously been done by the Unions; but the impartiality that the work required led to worker dissatisfaction which undermined the usefulness of the Unions as Mass Organisations. See, 'The report of the Ministry of Labour of the Central People's Government', *LT* 1950 No. 3, pp. 21–3.

[2] The 'simplification' drives were started in 1949, but until the budgetary cuts were made in early 1950 they were not very effective. See, 'Rely on the workers to simplify structure', *CFJP* 29 Jul. 1949 and 'Develop the simplification movement', *CFJP* 12 Aug. 1949.

said that he regarded unemployment as 'the most serious problem at present confronting the People's Government'.[1]

At the level of general policy, the Government attempted to relieve the situation by slackening the budgetary squeeze and by measures to encourage the expansion of the private sector. The Government also affirmed its decision to maintain the employment of 3 million persons in public administration and education and to delay demobilisation of the Kuomintang armies. Underlying these measures was the confidence that unemployment difficulties were a short-term phenomenon that would disappear under the impact of general economic advance, and we find that theorists at this time were still arguing that one of the main purposes of the Land Reform (which was then taking place) was to release rural labour for the towns.[2]

In addition to these general measures the Government issued directives on unemployment which stipulated that unemployment relief in the form of grain be given in the form of wages for public works and capital for the establishment of small-scale enterprises to be staffed by the unemployed. Other assistance was to be given to enable peasants to return to their villages and in the last resort, as pure relief. These forms of relief recur regularly during the 1950s, and for convenience we shall refer to them as the 'Four Ways'.[3] The criteria for receiving relief of any kind were however fairly strict. Only those who had lost employment *since* 1949 and who had no work or supplementary form of income of any kind were to benefit. As far as possible relief funds were to be raised by levies on enterprises and by workers in employment contributing a day's pay to the fund.

The administration of unemployment relief was in the hands of

[1] Mao Tse-tung, *Wei cheng ch'u kuo chia ts'ai cheng ching chi chi pen hao pien erh tou cheng* (Struggle for a basic improvement in our national economy and finances), (1950). Chou En-lai was responsible for the 1950 directives published in *HHYP* 1950 No. 7, p. 556. Ch'en Yi's speech is in *CFJP* 30 Jul. 1950.

[2] A good example of the optimistic view of employment prospects is 'The problem of unemployed workers', *Shanghai kung shang tzu liao* 4 Feb. 1950. The note on Land Reform is 'Why is Land Reform a pre-requisite for industrialisation', *HH* Ser. 1, No. 6, 25 Feb. 1950, p. 15.

[3] The 'Four Ways' and the standards for relief handouts in the early 1950s were closely anticipated by the Shanghai City Government prior to 1949. 'Unemployment relief in post war Shanghai', *SHYK* Ser. 2, No. 3, 5 Feb. 1947.

special committees under the Regional Military Governments and in practice, the Labour Bureaux. The Bureaux also alleviated unemployment by the establishment of special offices to register and find work for unemployed skilled workers, teachers and intellectuals.[1]

The reports of the Labour Ministry for 1949 and 1950 confirm that the Bureaux' main work in these years was mediation and unemployment. These issues were in practice closely related since one of the key areas of dispute, particularly in the private sector, was the issue of hiring and firing. This problem raised an awkward dilemma, for on the one hand the Government knew that capitalists had to keep costs under control to remain viable and that toleration of private enterprise implied some toleration of freedom in labour matters, yet on the other hand unemployment had to be controlled as far as possible. The job of reconciling these conflicting objectives constituted the main work of labour administration in this early period, and out of this work emerged the first sets of rules governing the hiring and firing of workers.

In February 1950, for example, the Labour Bureau in Shanghai affirmed that all sacking required Bureau agreement and after publication of the unemployment directives the Bureau added that, in principle, all hiring was to go through the Bureau as well. Thus the Bureau found itself in a complex position for we find that at the same time as the Bureau was dealing with illegal sackings in accordance with the unemployment directives, the Head of the Shanghai Labour Bureau was pointing out that realistic manning standards in the private sector were bound to involve some sacking.[2]

In 1951, however, the upturn of the urban economy presented the labour administrators with a new set of problems. Employment rose

[1] *Hua tung ch'ü ts'ai cheng ching chi fa ling hui pien* (1951), Vol. 2, pp. 1799–1827. For a retrospective view of unemployment directives see, Lan Chih, 'My country's unemployment relief and employment', *CCCP* No. 21, 29 May 1954, pp. 1–7.

[2] One loophole in these early rules was toleration of limited hiring of temporary workers who did not have to pass through any official machinery. In practice the regulations governing the use of these workers was widely ignored and in this way employers achieved more flexibility in labour force management than they would otherwise have had. 'Abstract of the work report of the Shanghai Municipality Labour Bureau', *LT* 1950 No. 1, pp. 15–16; *Directives on unemployment relief*, *CFJP* 20 Jun. 1950; 'Report on present Labour–Capital relations in Shanghai', *CFJP* 19 Oct. 1950; 'The Labour Bureau makes a timely reversal of illicit sackings at the New Life Shop', *CFJP* 16 Jun. 1950; 'Illegal hiring of temporary workers', *CFJP* 19 Jan. 1951.

very rapidly as is indicated in Table 32, and as unemployment decreased, the tensions and social problems associated with unemployment began to subside – and confidence in the long term prospects for urban employment was renewed.[1]

Table 32. *Numbers of registered unemployed in all urban areas, East China and Shanghai, 1950–51*

	(000's)		
	Mid-1950	End-1950	Mid-1951
All urban areas[a]	1,660	610	450
East China[b]	570	280	130
Shanghai[c]	170	n.a.	46

SOURCES:
[a] A report by Ch'en Yün reprinted in *Szu ying kung shang yeh ti she hui chu i kai tsao cheng ts'e fa ling hsüan pien 1953–1957* (Select compendium of policy statements and laws concerning the socialist reform of private industry and commerce), (1960).
[b] Ts'eng Shan 'Report on financial and economic work in East China', *CFJP* 27 Nov. 1951.
[c] '100,000 Shanghai workers return to production posts', *CFJP* 8 Jan. 1952.

The result of these developments was that the emphasis in the Bureaux' work switched from control of firing to control of hiring; and although the Union permission was still formally required, the right of employees to leave a job was affirmed and the right to fire was given a broader interpretation than had been the case in 1950.[2] Another effect of the increase in confidence was a broadening of the criteria for giving relief, and by December the Government was able to renew the programme of administrative simplification without fears of serious unemployment consequences.[3]

[1] There is evidence that social unrest was directly related to fluctuations in employment. For example, in Canton in mid-1950 there were reports of riots related to the intensification of unemployment. In Shanghai, the improvement in the employment situation in 1951 was reputed to have led to a sharp decrease in crime. '40,000 unemployed workers in Canton ask for work without result', *Hsing tao jih pao* (Hong Kong) 15 Jul. 1950; 'Robberies show a sharp decrease in Shanghai' *HWJP* 27 Aug. 1951 (*SCMP* 184).
[2] 'Recruitment of workers and job jumping serious problems in Shanghai', *CFJP* 11 Oct. 1951 (*SCMP* 212); 'The establishment of New Democratic Labour–Capital relations and current problems', *LT* 1951 Ser. II, No. 12, p. 11.
[3] 'Broaden the scope of unemployment relief', *CFJP* 20 Nov. 1950; 'Resolutely struggle against waste and corruption', *JMJP* 23 Nov. 1951.

Thus the real work of the Bureaux in 1951 was to control the effects of a tight labour market. For it was realised that shortages of skilled labour and the growth of unscrupulous and illicit hiring practices constituted a threat to the public sector which, in the 'era of planning' which lay ahead, could assume serious proportions. This led to the implementation of a new measure to control the flow of labour between the main administrative divisions and at the same time we begin to see demands appearing that in the long term the Bureaux should aim to establish a comprehensive machinery for controlling *all* employment decisions.[1]

These trends were abruptly reversed in the first half of 1952 when the labour market was again transformed; this time by the *san fan* and *wu fan* movements. These were attacks on bureaucracy and capitalism and were accompanied by a wave of sackings. The seriousness of the situation was reflected in repeated undertakings that workers who participated in the political work of these movements would be safe-guarded from victimisation and unemployment.[2] But these were largely empty promises and it is evident that the unemployment consequences of the *wu fan* movement were a major factor in bringing it to a halt in May 1952. By this time, however, urban unemployment was again high and confidence in the prospects for urban employment growth again shattered.[3] The seriousness of this collapse was intensified by the fact that the first round of agrarian cooperativisation had increased rural unemployment and accelerated the flow of peasants to the cities. The situation

[1] The regulations appear in *LT* 1950 No. 5 and *LT* 1951 No. 11. 'On the case for overall hiring see, Chiang To, 'The theoretical basis and fundamental tasks of unified labour allocation work', *CCCP* Ser. 13, No. 20, 15 Nov. 1951, pp. 386–7.

[2] Sackings and riots were reported in Canton, Chungking, Swatow, Chekiang and Wuhan. '30,000 unemployed', *Kung shang jih pao* (Industry and Commerce daily, hereafter *KSJP*), (Hong Kong) 16 Jun. 1952; 'Two-hundred unemployed Huan pottery workers demonstrate', *KSJP* 14 Oct. 1952; 'Correct the phenomenon of sacking workers and staff in the public and private sectors', *Chung ch'ing jih pao* (Chungking daily) 14 Oct. 1952; 'The city of Hangchow agrees on eight practical measures', *Che chiang jih pao* (Chekiang daily) 5 Feb. 1952; 'Unemployment relief work in Wuhan city during the past two years', *CCJP* 29 Sep. 1952.

[3] There are many reports that indicate lack of confidence in the Government's ability to solve urban unemployment problems in mid-1952. This pessimism was particularly widespread within Government organs as well as among the public at large. 'The Tientsin branch of the All China Federation of Trade Unions makes its reply', *T'ien chin jih pao* (Tientsin daily, hereafter *TCJP*) 2 Aug. 1952.

called for radical measures, and in the first instance these took the form of the employment *decisions* of 1952.

The 'decisions' on employment

These *decisions* were a major document in the sense that they constituted the first recognition that unemployment was a serious problem and would remain so in the medium term; they also acknowledged that unemployment had grown as a result of urban and rural economic reorganisation and was not simply a problem inherited from the Kuomintang. The *decisions* however were basically optimistic and although they emphasised that unemployment arising from structural reorganisation would continue, they foresaw rapid absorption of unemployed workers when the era of large-scale construction arrived. In the meantime, four lines of attack on the problem were proposed. These were: control of participation, the maintenance of redundant employees in employment, control of hiring and firing, and enlargement of the unemployment work of the Bureaux.[1] Let us consider these briefly in turn.

Control of participation concentrated on female participation and time. The question of working women was an extremely difficult one throughout our period. The demand to participate in the work force was considerable and the Party's experience of economic administration in wartime had convinced it of the potential value of women workers. Thus in the upswings of 1950–51, 1956 and 1958 particularly, we find positive efforts to encourage female participation.[2] Yet whenever the urban labour market contracted, the whole apparatus of persuasion and propaganda had to be mobilised in an effort to keep women out of the labour force. This is what happened in 1952, although it was emphasised that restriction on female participation was only a short-term measure which would be unnecessary when large-scale construction began.[3]

---

[1] *Decisions on the problem of employment, JMJP* 4 Aug. 1952.

[2] For 1950–51 see, *Ch'eng shih fu nü ts'an chia sheng ch'an ti ching yen* (Experience in facilitating the participation of urban women in production), (1950).

[3] See, Mao Tse-tung, *Ching chi wen t'i yü ts'ai cheng wen t'i* (Economic and financial problems), (1949) *passim* for appreciation of the value of female labour. After the directive

Control of working hours was not an entirely new departure. An eight-hour day was stated by Li Li-san in 1950 to be the long-term objective, although immediate implementation was thought at that time to be impracticable. By 1952, it was appreciated that employment considerations reinforced this long term, humanitarian view and a rigorous campaign was started to initiate two and three shift systems, each shift being normally of eight hours.[1] The Journal of the Labour Ministry, Lao tung (Labour), devoted an entire issue to this topic and quoted with approval an example of a factory where shift reform had resulted in a 74% increase in the labour force.[2]

The third aspect of participation, age, is one we know little about. It seems probable however, that age participation was also subject to further restriction around this time. For we know, that whereas Li Li-san was saying that in 1950 premature enforcement of restriction on child labour would be wrong, by 1955 a survey of the labour force in the public sector showed very small numbers of employees under the age of sixteen.

Control of redundancy unemployment had been started in 1949, relaxed in 1951 and renewed in late 1952. After the 1952 directive it had two aspects. First there was the question of redundancies arising from rationalisation in all sectors. The rule here was that redundant workers were to be kept on the pay roll until alternative work could be found.[3] Second, there was the question of the private sector, where the task of the Bureaux was much more delicate, for their task was to try to reverse the whole trend of sackings and encourage capitalists to begin hiring again.

These policies implied renewal of the attempt to control both

had been published the All China Women's Federation was mobilised to support the new limitations on female participation in the labour force. See 'The All China Women's Federation notifies all levels of the Federation to cooperate in the implementation of the Central People's Government, State Council's decisions on employment', *JMJP* 10 Aug. 1952.

[1] It was claimed that even prior to August 1952, the Party organisation had been fighting managers and capitalists to get multiple shift working introduced. See, 'The Party cares for workers welfare; settles a thousand unemployed in work', *NFJP* 1 May 1952.

[2] *LT* 1952 Vol. 11, No. 5.

[3] See the *Decisions*, as p. 97. An interesting discussion by the Head of the Shanghai Bureau on the policy of retention and instructions to the private sector are in *CFJP* 27 Aug. 1952 and *CFJP* 17 Aug. 1952. The Unions were also instructed to encourage private sector hiring and control of time participation, *CFJP* 2 Dec. 1952.

hiring and firing. The latter was particularly important since the Bureaux' power in this respect had suffered some attenuation in 1951. However, care had to be taken that the new rules were not applied too rigidly to the private sector, since if, in effect, hiring was made irreversible, this would act as powerful disincentive to potential employers – particularly those engaged in businesses where labour requirements tended to fluctuate seasonally.[1]

The *decisions* resulted in considerably increased activity for the Bureaux and to some extent in increased prestige. There was certainly scope for improvement in the administration of unemployment which was thoroughly overhauled at this time.[2] The earlier unemployment directive had been intrinsically difficult to administer and had suffered from failure of the Bureaux to allocate administrative resources to unemployment work. Criteria for registration were too narrow and the formalities of registration were too complex. Moreover, we have to realise that throughout the 1950s there was a widespread and justified fear of registration of any kind which the 1950 directive did nothing to alleviate.[3]

To overcome these problems the scope of the registration was broadened, formalities simplified and the new round of registration was accompanied by a large-scale propaganda campaign.[4] These measures had some success. Indeed too much, for they led to a widespread exodus from low income occupations in rural and urban areas by persons hoping that unemployment registration might

[1] See the *Decisions* and an explanatory article, 'Problems of employment', *JMJP* 16 Sep. 1952. One extraordinarily tricky area of hiring control was that of small-scale firms that changed the character of their business. This sort of trade switching was frequently a device to shed unwanted employees and the Labour Bureaux had to keep an eye on these situations and judge the employment implications of each case on its merits.

[2] Accounts of embezzlement of unemployment funds and various forms of maladministration are numerous, see for example *TCJP* 6 Jan. 1952, *CCHHJP* 18 Apr. 1951, *JMJP* 24 Mar. 1952, *Hsi an ch'ün chung jih pao* (Sian Masses Daily) 10 Oct. 1952. An authoritative account of the confusion which arose as the result of the multiplication of types of registration is 'Report on unemployment work in 1950', *LT* 1951 No. 7, pp. 4–6.

[3] Fear of registration for employment and other purposes was based on the role played by the Public Security organs in this work and this persisted at least until 1955, when Shanghai Roman Catholics were still reported as saying that: 'Unemployment registration is a sugar-coated artillery pill', *HWJP* 9 Sep. 1955, translated in *URI Research Service Series*, 27. Sep. 1955, No. 4.

[4] *Methods for unemployment registration, JMJP* 20 Aug. 1952.

prove the most direct route to new and more attractive work in the public sector.[1]

For most of those who were put on the register however, the prospects remained those of the 'Four Ways', although these were interpreted more liberally and underwritten with more substantial assistance than previously.[2]

There were two other new developments in the Bureaux' work connected with the *decisions*. The first was that unemployment work and the work of assignment and introduction were linked firmly together; for efficient settlement of the unemployed was seen to depend on a general submission to Labour Bureau job-finding procedures.[3]

The other change brought by the decisions was the reversal of Li Li-san's definition of the Bureaux' relations with the private sector. The key word in 1950 had been mediation. In 1952, as a result of a bitter struggle in the *wu fan* campaign, it was changed to partisanship; a change that must have hindered the Bureaux in their efforts to increase employment in the private sector.[4]

The changes in the employment situation brought about by the measures to stimulate the urban economy in mid-1952, and by the employment decisions, were all considered as short term palliatives. In the longer run, a programme of rapid industrialisation was seen as the solution to urban employment problems. Moreover, even

[1] For example, 'Gradually and by plan strive to do employment work well', *CFJP* 11 Sep. 1952. In Peking and Chungking it was reported that on hearing of the employment decisions, peasants surrendered their land to local peasant associations and with cadre assistance moved into the cities, *CFJP* 11 Sep. 1952.

[2] The 'return to the countryside' in 1952 was not quite what was intended in the 1950 regulations. In 1950 the problem had been primarily that of returning recent refugees to the countryside; in 1952, the emphasis was on the possibility of absorbing labour in rural areas by a positive policy of land reclamation.

[3] An explicit statement of the principle that choice of job would not be possible before full employment is in 'Questions and answers on employment', *TCJP* 29 Oct. 1952.

[4] The *wu fan* (five antis) had a traumatic effect on the Labour Ministry and its Bureaux. No issue of the Ministry's official Journal *Lao tung* appeared between November 1951 and September 1952, when it re-emerged with the new employment decisions. The struggle in the Bureaux was between three groups, those who argued that the Bureaux should defend capitalists; those who argued for impartiality in the context of the political theory of the 'bloc of four classes'; and those who wanted the Bureaux to support the workers. See, 'Correct rightist thought tendencies in the workers movement in private factories in An Tung', *JMJP* 7 Feb. 1952.

the longer run was thought of as a period of only three to five years and it is plausible that the timing of the plan itself may have been brought forward in the light of the unemployment situation in late 1952 – for there is evidence that there were many who regarded the decision to launch a major effort in 1953 as both premature and dangerous. Yet without such a plan in immediate prospect, the reasoning of the *decisions* would largely fall to the ground, since once the upswing had brought the economy to full capacity in late 1952, the prospects for subsequent employment growth would be poor.[1]

[1] A period of three to five years was specifically mentioned for the solution of the unemployment problem in East China, 'East China holds an employment conference', *CFJP* 16 Aug. 1952. If the First Plan was brought forward in the light of employment considerations this would constitute a parallel with Soviet experience. See, Margaret Dewar, *Labour policy in the U.S.S.R. 1917–1928* (1956), p. 156 and Isaac Deutscher, *The Soviet trade unions* (1950), pp. 67–8.

6

FIRST STEPS IN EMPLOYMENT PLANNING, 1953–55

THE EMPLOYMENT STRATEGY OF THE FIRST FIVE YEAR PLAN

In the closing months of 1952 the urban economy began to warm up for the First Five Year Plan. We do not know what rate of industrial and construction growth had originally been planned for 1953, but since we know that the construction plan was cut twice early in the year and still achieved an increase in output of 66%, the presumption must be that the earlier control figures were very high indeed.[1] Similarly, we do not know what rates of growth were envisaged for the whole of the First Plan period. The final version of the Plan which appeared in July 1955 had been scaled down in 1953 and 1955, and even this version had a planned rate of industrial growth of 14·8%. This seems to indicate that in late 1952, when plans were still very ambitious, it was hoped that China's First Plan would have output and employment growth rates of the order of magnitude of those in the First Russian Plan.[2] With such a plan the Chinese expected to achieve full urban employment and net labour transfer from the rural sector. For in Russia, industrial employment had grown at 15·9% per annum in the First and Second Plans, and during the initial burst from 1929 to 1932 the industrial labour force increased from 3·1 to 8 millions. Two-thirds of the entrants to the urban labour force in these years came from the rural areas so that between 1926 and 1939 the urban population more than doubled its absolute size and increased its share of total population from 17·9% to 32·8%.[3]

---

[1] *TCKT* 1954 No. 7, p. 3.

[2] The planned rate of industrial growth in the First Russian Plan rose during the course of the Plan period from 21·4% to 25·2% per annum. Views on the extent to which the Plan fulfilled its aims vary. Hodgeman estimates that annual growth rate of industry between 1927/8–1933 was 11·5%. The official index claims a rate of 18·5% See data in Schwartz, p. 136.

[3] Data from Harry Schwartz, pp. 32 and 521; Solomon M. Schwarz, *Labour in the Soviet Union* (1953); S. Swaniewicz, *Forced labour and economic development* (1965), p. 150.

Why did the Chinese think that they could emulate the Russian performance? One reason was the general supposition that, since before 1917 Russia like China had been a backward, semi-feudal, and asiatic country, what had been achieved in the one should be possible to the other. A second factor was the experience of Manchuria, where even before 1949 there had been an industrial transformation sufficient to produce some net inter-sectoral labour transfers, and where by 1952, there were high levels of urban employment and some absorption of labour from rural Manchuria as well as from other parts of China.[1] In the First Plan period, Manchurian experience was repeatedly described as following a pattern that would be extended to the rest of the Chinese economy – what had happened in Manchuria between 1948 and 1952 was confidently expected to be the general case between 1953 and 1957. A third consideration which may have served to underwrite an optimistic view of the Plan's prospects, was the national economic performance between 1949 and 1952. During this period industry had grown at 34·6% per annum and industrial employment at 19·8%.[2] It was therefore tempting to think that if the limitations of existing capacity and other objective constraints could somehow be released by 'planning' and 'socialisation', the economy might be able to maintain a performance of the order reached in the recovery period.

The validity of this reconstruction of Chinese expectations in late 1952 is borne out, not only by the specific expectations of the *decisions on employment*, but also by the literature on the population problem which appeared in some profusion in 1953 as a by-product of the preparation of the first national census. We can illustrate this by reference to an article typical of those published at this time.[3] In this article the view that China was 'over-populated' was discussed with close reference to employment issues and dismissed on

[1] According to Chang Ch'en-ta, between 1934 and 1944 the rural population of Manchuria declined from 84·7% to 67·4% of the total population, see Chang Chen-ta, *Tung pei ching chi* (The economy of north east China), (1954), pp. 24–5. For a typical view of Manchurian employment experience and its relevance see 'The number of employed persons in the North East has increased enormously', *NFJP* 25 Sep. 1952.

[2] Emerson (1965), table 1. Industrial production is the official index, *Ten great years*, p. 87.

[3] Yen Chien-yü, 'From a few population questions discuss the great significance of the population census', *Hsin chien she* (New construction, hereafter *HCS*) 1953 No. 5.

several grounds. First, the author argued that the static concept of a 'normal' population was inadequate in a world where production relations could be changed with immediate, positive effects on production. Second, he pointed out that *in the plan period* the Soviet Union had eliminated unemployment, and secured radical redistribution of population between the rural and urban areas. Third, the article argued for an optimistic view of employment prospects on the grounds that, 'the last three years show that the surplus population concept is rubbish'.

And finally, apart from industry, the article claimed that there was scope for employment absorption in agriculture, where the cooperativisation movement would generate employment in secondary occupations and where there were further possibilities in the programme for land reclamation. Thus it is worth noting that by 1953, although confidence in the prospects for industrial employment was still high, agricultural cooperatives are already being thought of as instruments to increase total employment, rather than as controls through which labour was to be supplied to the urban areas.

THE WORK OF THE BUREAUX IN 1953: THE BEGINNINGS OF MANPOWER PLANNING

At the national level, the work of the Labour Ministry in 1953 was modest in scope. For although manpower planning in Manchuria was already quite advanced, the economic reports for 1952 and 1953 both suggest that there was no comprehensive, national labour plan in those years.[1]

The 1952 plan was particularly limited and the labour data quoted in the plan's out-turn were confined to the numbers of workers and staff in state economic departments and productivity increases in centrally controlled industrial enterprises. The 1953 out-turn, however, suggests a widening of interests since it included data on all workers and staff broken down in some detail, and productivity and real wage data for workers in the public sector industry. But in

[1] 'State Statistical Bureau report for 1952', *Kung shang chieh* (The world of private industry and commerce) No. 7, pp. 38–42; 'State Statistical Bureau report for 1953', *TCKT* 1954 No. 7, pp. 1–8.

neither of these reports were out-turn data compared with any plan, whereas industrial output and other important indicators were.

This absence of comprehensive manpower plans at the national level means that any planning that took place must have been at the local and ministerial levels, and that these plans were either too unreliable or too untimely to make a more comprehensive plan possible.

In the absence of formal central planning, the work of the Bureaux in 1953 consisted largely of trying to control hiring and of satisfying the demand for labour in the public sector as it arose. Primarily, this involved organising the labour supply for departments with the fastest planned rates of growth – above all, basic construction.[1]

Basic construction work involved both training workers and developing effective means of directly controlling and allocating the construction labour force. This proved extremely difficult. First, because high levels of urban employment meant that dissatisfied workers could escape official assignment and find alternative work. Second, because construction management cadres, faced with work loads nearly twice as high as 1952, were prepared to ignore and circumvent the planned assignment apparatus if this was necessary to ensure fulfilment of physical output targets. And third, because the Government abolished the old work gang system (*pao t'ou chih*) which had the effect of atomising the construction labour market.[2] This last point is of considerable importance. There was a case on both social and economic grounds for the elimination of the construction job brokers. But in the short term this made control of the work force extremely difficult and the machinery that was established in the construction industry between 1953 and 1955 was, in some ways, a functional substitute for the old system.[3]

[1] 'Main tasks of the Central Government Ministry of Labour 1953 work plan', *LT* 1953 No. 3, p. 9.
[2] There was a particularly severe construction labour crisis in the North East in early 1953 which followed the abolition of the *pao t'ou chih* in 1952. *TPJP* 10 Jan. 1953; *TPJP* 13 Apr. 1953.
[3] The *pao t'ou chih* was also abolished in the traditional transport sector, but in this case it did not lead to any problems. The reason for this was that unemployment in this sector meant that the workers were in no position to frustrate plans made for them by labour administrators.

The main feature of the new system of construction labour control – following the Manchurian model – was a set of rules for registration and introduction. These were supported by the establishment of local 'Labour Balancing Committees' in areas where the work involved was considered to be too great to be handled by the Bureaux alone. These Committees had representatives of all parties interested in labour supply and they attempted to match local supply and demand of construction labour.[1]

In the event of net excesses of demand or supply, balancing Committees in different areas could cooperate with each other to secure inter-regional balance. The one overriding principle in the work of the Committees was that they had to operate within a framework of priorities determined by the Government.[2]

The effective operation of the Committees required a continued effort by the Bureaux to control all hiring and also the introduction of new powers to order inter-enterprise transfers of personnel where this seemed necessary.[3]

These developments in 1953 took hiring control a step nearer to labour planning because the demands made for construction labour were so great that in the search for realistic criteria for ordering local construction priorities the Bureaux were forced to devise rules of thumb for the conversion of planned work loads into labour requirements. In other words, the Bureaux began to take a detailed interest in labour administration at the enterprise level.[4]

It is difficult to assess the success of this work in 1953, but the evidence of local case studies is that it was slight. One report, for example, analysed the out-turn of the labour plan of a large construction enterprise in Anshan. This revealed that actual labour require-

---

[1] *NFJP* 25 Sep. 1952; *LT* 1953 Nos. 2 and 10 have particularly relevant materials on this.

[2] The priorities for allocating labour were: (1) defence, (2) industry, (3) 'ordinary', (4) repair: 'A summary of unified allocation of construction workers in Tientsin', LT 1953 No. 2, p. 9.

[3] Skilled construction workers required for special construction enterprises were frequently employed by large industrial enterprises who did much of their own construction and who vigorously resisted attempts to strip them of their personnel. See, 'The experience of the Anshan Iron and Steel Company in transferring cadres from the production department to build up the basic construction work force to full strength', *JMJP* 11 Dec. 1952.

[4] *CFJP* 17 Jan. 1953.

ments had exceeded the plan by 34%; that the number of staff employed exceeded the number indicated by official norms by 58%; and that the productivity plan had fallen short by 34%. This suggests that enterprise level planning in the construction industry was still at a 'bacchanalian' stage.[1]

Closely connected to the Bureaux' work in construction and employment control was a new role in the control of general population movements. In spring 1953, the upswing of construction in the towns and the general optimism surrounding the introduction of the Five Year Plan, combined with grain shortages in the rural areas to stimulate a large flow of peasants into the cities. The authorities attempted to control this influx by directives, but in autumn, the poor harvest and widespread natural catastrophies led to a renewed inflow. Construction and illicit hiring both served to facilitate this migration and recognition of this was one of the motives behind the general tightening of employment control in late 1953.

THE RENEWED EMPLOYMENT CRISIS: AUTUMN 1953 TO AUTUMN 1955

The two years between the end of the 'Leap Forward' of 1953 and the 'High Tide' in the countryside in autumn 1955 have been comparatively neglected by students of China's economy. This period tends either to be ignored or subsumed in an analysis of the whole First Plan period. This is unfortunate, since it was precisely the inability of the Government to solve the problems of the First Plan within the institutional framework as it operated in these years, that led to the cycle of radical upheavals which lasted from late 1955 to the Great Leap Forward in 1958. The reasoning behind these upheavals cannot be understood without reference to the problems which seemed insoluble within the rules of the institutional system they largely destroyed. Here, we are concerned with only one aspect of this. But our analysis of the crisis in labour work is probably indicative of what could be found in other sectors.

[1] 'An initial analysis of management in 1953', *TCKT* 1954 No. 4. The term 'bacchanalian' was used by Naum Jasny to describe the planning of the early Stalinist period, Naum Jasny, *Soviet industrialization* (1961).

In employment work, the crucial issue was the slowdown of employment absorption. Indeed by 1955 it is probable that in the construction, commerce and services sectors substantial disabsorption was taking place.[1] These developments contradicted the expectations generated by the 1952 employment *decisions* and the early drafts of the Plan and we have to ask, therefore, why it was that two years after the implementation of a Plan expected to lead to the rapid elimination of urban unemployment, unemployment was visibly increasing.

The first miscalculation arose from false analogies between China and the Soviet Union. For it seems probable that the planners allowed some real similarities of political history and social strucure to obscure differences in resource endowment and the size of the initial industrial and employment base that were of critical relevance to the formulation of economic plans. These differences made long run growth rates of the order achieved by the Soviet Union unrealistic for the Chinese *on almost any assumptions* about the prospects for foreign assistance; and implied employment absorption of a lower order, even had very high rates of industrial output growth been achieved. For the speed and character of employment reallocation depends on the initial structure of the work force and the speed at which its components are changing; and if the initial base of industrial employment is minute, even rapid growth of industrial employment will have to be sustained over a very long period before any significant transformation has taken place. If we take employment in industry as a percentage of total population as an indicator of the initial base, comparison between Russia and China indicates how backward the latter was. In Russia in 1926 (three years before the First Plan), employment in large-scale industry was equal to 1·9% of total population; for China, in 1949, the figures range between 0·2% and 0·5% depending on one's choice of data.[2]

[1] The construction labour force declined in 1954 and 1955, and in the trade and food sectors we estimate a net loss of 1,462,000 jobs between the end of 1953 and 1955. This is based on data for the private sector in *Szu ying shang yeh ti she hui chu i kai tsao* (*tzu liao*) and Emerson, (1965) table 3.
[2] Soviet data from Schwarz, *Labour in the Soviet Union*. Chinese data from *Ten great years*, p. 183 and Wu Yuan-li *An economic survey of Communist China* (1956), p. 37.

The employment implications of this difference were intensified by the fact that whereas the growth of labour productivity in the First Russian Plan was low, in China the overall national figure for productivity growth was quite high. Thus whereas in Russia increasing capital intensity was offset by slow productivity growth, in China it was not.[1] The Chinese Plan as implemented in these years had other implications that were prejudicial to urban employment growth. We saw in Chapter 1 the way in which the rigid and over-centralised finance system designed to guarantee the supply of resources necessary for the key-point projects had a deadening effect on other forms of economic activity. The consequences of this for employment were disproportionately severe because fiscal strictness bore particularly hard on locally-managed construction and small-scale activities, both of which were fairly labour intensive. And it is notable that we have one directive for these years which indicates that even where mild budgetary relaxation was allowed, there was a specific instruction that the relaxation was not to be used to hire additional personnel in the public sector.[2]

A further aspect of the concentration of resources in key public sector projects was that it implied a repressive policy against the private sector, and in 1954 and 1955 the effects of this were compounded by unforseen factors such as the conclusion of the Korean war. The decline in the level of activity in the private sector had disproportionate effects on employment, since small-scale businesses under pressure, rid themselves of labour, not only because in the face of uncertain prospects they were reluctant to accept long term obligations to their employees, but also because they wished to avoid being classified as capitalists and thereby laying themselves open to direct political pressures of the most unpleasant character. In urban commerce, for example, enterprises with *two or more* employees were classified as capitalist and therefore liable to 'reform' rather than cooperativisation. As there were many enterprises

[1] Chinese data from Chapter 3. Soviet data from Naum Jasny, *Soviet industrialization*, pp. 104-8. According to the latter, labour productivity in large-scale industry fell about 35% to 40% between 1929 and 1932 – years of exceptional employment growth.

[2] 'Carry through the policy of finance work being subordinated to production', *NFJP* 24 Apr. 1954.

near this limit, it is not surprising to find that the decline of *hired* labour in commerce between 1953 and 1955 was more rapid than the decline of *total* employment in that sector.[1]

The drive to reduce budgetary expenditure in 1954 and 1955 also led to a renewed round of manpower rationalisation in the public sector. This affected all categories of employment and was a specific reversal of the policy of the 1952 employment *decisions* which had required the indefinite retention of personnel made redundant by increased productivity.

The main drive for rationalisation began in April 1955; and in July of that year there was an important conference of Labour Bureau chiefs in which the role of the Bureaux in this campaign was worked out.[2] The main emphasis in this campaign was on persons not engaged directly in productive work, and the size of the manpower excess which had built up in the early 1950s is indicated by reports that in some departments only two-thirds of the office staff had any meaningful activity, and that in the Anshan iron and steel complex only 52·3% of the total labour force was actually engaged in production. We also have a revealing series of employment and turnover data for the Kansu commerce sector which show how productivity declined in the First Plan period.[3] Thus although measurement of productivity change is notoriously difficult in work outside productive departments, there can be little doubt that the employment *decisions* and the cyclical mechanism analysed in Chapter 4 had resulted in substantial overmanning, and that in 1954 and 1955 the situation was aggravated by both pressures from below to increase employment in the public sector to offset disabsorption elsewhere, and by the unwillingness or inability of economic and bureaucratic organisations to resist these.

The campaign to control the growth of non-productive labour took two forms. First, there was an attempt to devise standard structures of work differentiation which could be applied throughout an

[1] The data on the decline in hired men are for all areas, see Ch'ien Hua and others (1957), table 2, p. 9.

[2] 'The Labour Chiefs emphasise the importance of labour management and similar problems', *JMJP* 17 Jul. 1955.

[3] *JMJP* 17 Jul. 1955; *HHPYK* 1957 No. 2, pp. 87–9; 'A serious waste of manpower in the Anshan Iron and Steel Company', *KJJP* 1 Apr. 1955; *KSJP* 1 Apr. 1958.

administrative or industrial system. The model for this type of work was the railway system, which had borrowed its personnel structure from the Soviet railway system.[1]

The second form of attack was the drive to enforce retirement. The lack of retirement in accordance with the insurance regulations had reached serious proportions by 1955, and constituted an unplanned and wholly unwelcome increase in the participation rate. One problem was that the regulations had the force of law only for a minority of enterprises and thus we have one report that suggests that in Shanghai in the late 1950s only about one-third of the urban work force was eligible to retire under the provisions of the labour insurance law. In addition, the regulation in force in the mid-1950s actually provided monetary incentives to workers who stayed on after fulfilling the conditions for retirement, in that such workers were entitled not only to draw their existing pay, but to draw supplements of a further 10% to 20% as well. It is not surprising therefore to find that a survey of Shanghai cigarette factories found that 57% of those eligible to retire refused to do so.[2]

In 1955, the Labour Bureaux were called upon to implement new retirement rules for state administrative organs and to devise alternative work and income arrangements attractive and credible enough to make workers generally willing to leave their unproductive positions in the public sector. Given the depressed state of the urban economy in 1955 this was impossible.

The third aspect of this campaign to control public sector employment was a renewed drive in 1955 to stop net new hiring and to ensure that any additional labour requirements in the public sector were met through the reassignment of existing workers and staff.

Apart from specific directives on the subject of hiring control, by 1955 an apparatus had been built up that enabled the authorities to sound a new note of harshness in labour administration. In late 1953

[1] *LT* 1955 No. 6 and *LT* 1955 No. 11.

[2] The retirement rules under the 1951 and 1953 insurance regulations are in *Labour insurance regulations of the People's Republic of China* (1952), and *Important labour laws and regulations of the People's Republic of China* (1961). The 1955 regulations for employees in Government organs are in *Chung Hua jen min kung ho kuo fa kuei hui pien*, No. 2 (1956). Shanghai data are from *CFJP* 12 Apr. 1957; *CFJP* 28 Sep. 1956; *LT* 1957 No. 3, pp. 2-3.

there were the first important directives on labour discipline, and in 1954 the power of managements was greatly strengthened by the introduction of formalised rules to govern intra-enterprise work organisation. In retrospect these regulations were seen to provide the legal basis of hiring control.[1]

So far we have confined ourselves to considering the demand for labour. In conclusion we have to note two special factors on the supply side that accentuated the unemployment problem in this period. The first was the acceleration of migration into the towns between 1953 and 1955. This occurred in waves which were related to bad harvests, natural disasters, cooperativisation drives and the reorganisation of agricultural taxation. The degree of irreversibility in these migrations seemed to be rising all the time, and by spring 1955 Shanghai's total population reached a peak of 7,000,000, a figure which was not touched again until 1957. A second factor was the general demobilisation of the army which took place in 1955. This had been deliberately delayed in 1950 for employment considerations and these had subsequently been overtaken by the Korean War. By 1955, however, substantial disabsorption from the armed forces could not be delayed longer.[2]

From this account it can be seen that the context of labour administration in this period was one of increasing unemployment and also of deepening gloom. Let us now try to analyse the reaction of the Bureaux to this and the character of their work in these years.

THE WORK OF THE LABOUR BUREAUX, 1954–55

During 1954 and most of 1955 there was still nothing at the national level that could be described as overall manpower planning. This is confirmed by a revealing self-criticism that the Labour Ministry

[1] *Decisions on labour discipline*, *HHYP* 1953 No. 47, *An outline of inter-enterprise regulations for state enterprises*, *KMJP* 14 Jul. 1954. These latter regulations included the rule that employees could not leave their work without permission and in 1955 an article on labour control commented that: 'those who without reason refuse to submit to assignment should be punished', 'Strengthen labour force management and assignment work', *LT* 1955 No. 7, pp. 3–4. For a retrospective view of labour legislation, see, 'The great achievements in the establishment of labour law cannot be easily denied', *LT* 1958 No. 2, pp. 29–30.

[2] John Gittings, *The role of the Chinese army* (1967), pp. 96–7.

made in 1954. In this, the backwardness of the Ministry's work was contrasted with the development of industrial planning, and the unreality of manpower planning was such that it was admitted that 'we are still only at the stage of shouting, and even our shouting is feeble'.[1]

At the level of the Bureaux, however, there was plenty of activity. The most significant feature of their work in these years was the continuing attempt to intensify hiring control in basic construction and the public sector; while at the same time *relaxing control* in other sectors in an attempt to relieve unemployment. This mixed strategy was particularly in evidence in 1954, the first year of a new phase in employment policy. This policy was announced after a conference in March 1954 at which the errors of the 1952 *decisions* on employment were discussed and publicised.[2] At this conference it was admitted that the long-term character of the employment problem had not been appreciated and that the hopes of a solution to unemployment through expansion of construction had been ill founded. The conference also agreed that it had been a mistake to absorb unnecessary personnel into the public sector and that restriction on hiring in the private sector had been wrong. The training programme, the public works brigades, the relief factories and the policy of relating construction assignment and unemployment work were all subject to examination and found to have been unsuccessful or inefficient. A new approach was clearly called for and the first reform was that in future there would be *no* attempt to link unemployment work with overall control of hiring. Second, it was agreed that the scope of labour assignment should be sharply reduced so that the unemployed could use their own initiative to find work. This implied considerable relaxation of hiring rules and amounted to official encouragement of a licit free market in labour.[3]

---

[1] *LT* 1954 No. 10, pp. 10-11.

[2] Hsing Tzu-hung, 'Strive to continue implementation of the new employment policy', *HHYP* 1954 No. 7, pp. 141-2.

[3] The Shanghai regulations appear in *WHP* 28 Jun. 1954. See also articles in *SCMP* 984, 22 Sep. 1954. Although the regulations left some restrictions on hiring by economic enterprises; article 7 stated that 'administrative organs, public organisations, schools, hospitals and armed forces (not including subsidiary business enterprises of administrative organs and military supplies production departments) are free to engage employees and workers by themselves'.

In practice the new policy led to the abandonment of the whole apparatus of unemployment administration built up after the 1952 decisions, and it is significant that unemployment work *did not even appear* in the list of tasks for Labour Ministry work in 1954.[1] There can be little doubt that the Bureaux were thoroughly glad to be rid of a problem that they were powerless to resolve.

However at the same time as the Bureaux were relaxing control in one direction, other factors required that occupations and sectors still officially within the sphere of work assignment be subject to even tighter control than before. We have already seen that tighter control of hiring was implied by the new drive on waste in the public sector in 1955 and that the objectives of cost minimisation and population control required renewed effort in basic construction labour force management. Construction labour control in 1953 had been a disaster for the Bureaux, since they had failed completely to devise a control system which would enable the sector to build a stable, flexible work force with a rising skill level. Instead, there had been excessive use of unskilled, temporary labour which had been an unnecessary burden on costs and facilitated illicit migration. Moreover, the situation was in danger of deterioration because the vacuum of authority left by the abolition of the traditional job brokers was being filled by the leaders of new, informally organised groups – usually based on skill affinities. This threatened to complicate construction management still further.[2] As a result of all this, in 1954 and 1955 the Bureaux got really tough. Construction teams were organised on a local basis; universal registration was enforced; and workers who refused to accept assignment were subject to punishments and criticism, if necessary in courts of law.[3] In 1955 the grip of the authorities was tightened further as a result of a detailed check up of the work force in which the work of the

[1] In 1955, we have evidence that two cities stopped collection of the unemployment fund. See *CCJP* 3 Jan. 1955 and *KJJP* (Peking) 26 May 1955.

[2] 'Some views on improving site labour organisation', *LT* 1954 No. 4, pp. 14–15.

[3] See, 'The system for managing the temporary assignment of temporary construction workers in Tientsin', *LT* 1954 No. 10, pp. 40–1. 'Discussion on the problems of registering temporary construction workers', *LT* 1954 No. 10, pp. 27–8. Also Mao Ch'i-hua's report, 'Do well the work of allocating construction workers and subordinate [it] to national basic construction', *HHPYK* 1954 No. 7, pp. 138–40.

Labour Bureaux was actually merged with that of the Public Security organs.[1]

Despite some success in the construction industry, the problems facing the Bureaux were becoming increasingly intractable during the first eight months of 1955. For on the one hand pressure on the private and traditional sectors was increasing total unemployment, yet on the other, the Bureaux seemed incapable of controlling hiring and the retirement of personnel in the public sector.[2] One fundamental explanation of the latter phenomenon was the lack of power of local Bureaux, particularly over centrally controlled units. This had its origins in the 1950 directives that failed to provide them with the authority necessary for effective intervention in basic level employment administration. By 1955, this weakness was an insuperable obstacle to the fulfilment of a task which the Bureaux were unable to shed.[3] Another reason for the continued growth of bureaucratic employment appears to have been the incapacity of the leadership of these organisations to control the hiring activities of their basic level cadres even when they wished to do so – as appears to be the case in 1955. The multiplication of levels of authority and the confused relationships between coordinating bodies at each level of the geographical hierarchy, resulted in leakage of authority so substantial that lower level cadres were able to hire at will and thus indulge in what has been called 'bureaucratic free enterprise'.[4] Finally, one other factor that complicated hiring control in this period was the necessity, already mentioned, of relaxing hiring control in some sectors to minimise unemployment caused by inflexible controls and the Bureaux' incapacity to keep adequately informed of job opportunities. This led directly to the growth of licit free labour markets, and indirectly to the growth of illicit ones. Thus the experi-

[1] 'Struggle to liquidate every hidden counter-revolutionary', *LT* 1955 No. 9, pp. 1-2.
[2] 'Improve labour organisation to fulfil the 1955 labour plan', *LT* 1955 No. 1, pp. 13-14; 'Strengthen labour force management and assignment work', *LT* 1955 No. 7, pp. 3-4.
[3] In the Labour Ministry's Journal during this period there are some extremely funny cartoons illustrating disregard for the Bureaux' hiring regulations. A common theme is a house (representing an enterprise) with a Labour Bureau regulation forbidding additional hiring pinned to a closed front door; meanwhile dozens of workers and staff are pouring in by side entrances and through the windows.
[4] For a full exploration of this concept see, Gordon Tullock, *The politics of bureaucracy* (Washington: Public Affairs Press: 1965), pp. 167-70.

ence of this period suggests that however plausible in theory, the attempt to divide the urban labour market into free and controlled sectors was unworkable in practice.

Mid-1955 was a turning point in labour work as in economic policy in general and in the second half of that year we begin to see the emergence of new solutions to all these problems. Within the urban areas, the Bureaux began to press again for overall control of hiring, even (by implication) at the expense of increased unemployment. For not only had the Bureaux come to recognise the intrinsic unworkableness of a partially free labour market, but at the national level the Ministry of Labour, armed with the results of the 1955 survey of the labour force in the public sector, was anxious to construct more ambitious and comprehensive labour plans whose implementation required more comprehensive power, particularly over the private sector.[1]

By mid-1955, however, the urban unemployment problem had become intolerable and a downward revision of public sector labour requirements for the second half of the year would, had other things remained equal, have made it worse. But this was not to be the case, for throughout 1955 we find a new emphasis on the role of the agricultural sector in labour absorption and in the summer of 1955 we have the first round of the *hsia fang* (sending down) campaign.

This campaign to return large numbers of immigrants to the countryside was conceived on an ambitious scale and prosecuted with vigour. In Shanghai, for example, the original plan was to reduce the city's population by 1,000,000 (14%) although the final out-turn was only half that number.[2] Most of those who were 'sent down' were to go to the rural areas, although at the same time plans were made to send workers to other cities. Every medium of persuasion and a wide variety of material, normative and coercive inducements were utilised to make the campaign a success. The main emphasis of the campaign was on the importance of securing a voluntary return and the newspapers of the period are filled with letters from returned workers who affirmed the availability of food

[1] *JMJP* 17 Jul. 1955; *LT* 1955 No. 8, pp. 2–4.
[2] 'An important measure in Shanghai Municipality', *JMJP* 3 May 1955; *CFJP* 3 Aug. 1955.

and work, appealed to the nostalgia of migrant peasants and described with optimism the present and imminent changes in rural life which the cooperativisation was bringing about.

But there was something of a paradox in all this. For how could the employment problems of millions of urban residents be solved by a return to a cooperativised countryside when nearly all the evidence suggested that, prior to 1955, rural reform had *not* been favourable to increases in rural employment, but on the contrary had tended to diminish it? This consideration makes it probable that there was a close connection between the decision to launch the *hsia fang* movement and the decision to radicalise the rural cooperativisation movement in 1955; for only such radicalisation could lead to a genuinely comprehensive reorganisation of rural life that could make the planned expansion of rural employment feasible.

7

HIGH TIDE, CRISIS AND REFORM, 1956–57

EMPLOYMENT ASPECTS OF THE 'HIGH TIDE OF SOCIALISM',
1955–56

In late 1955, the Party launched a vigorous round of agricultural cooperativisation and the plans show that this was expected to have a dramatic impact on the urban economy and to retrieve the First Five Year Plan from the possibility of failure. But it is important to appreciate that the original plans for sharp increases in construction and industrial output in 1956 did not involve an immediate change in the employment strategies of 1955. This is confirmed by article 39 of the Twelve Year Plan for Agricultural Development (January 1956), which stated that the growth envisaged by the Plan would enable agriculture to absorb sufficient urban unemployment to enable the urban areas to achieve full employment within five to seven years. And, indeed, there is evidence that in early 1956 many cities were active in setting up agricultural cooperatives to absorb their unemployed manpower and surplus population.[1] Further confirmation of the continuity with the policies of 1955 is a series of revealing articles in the control figures for the 1956 Plan published in September 1955. Although these articles do not quote figures (since these would still be the subject of negotiation), they make it clear that the planners were envisaging that the planned increases of output were to be achieved by redistribution of the existing urban labour force and by a general increase in work intensity. And since 1956 was the first year in which there could be said to have been even an attempt at an overall labour plan, there was some reason to

[1] *The Draft Programme for Agricultural Development 1956–1967*, translated in Robert R. Bowie and John K. Fairbank, *Communist China 1955–1959: Policy documents and analysis* (1962), pp. 119–26; 'Changchun city sends more than 25,000 people to participate in agricultural production', *KMJP* 29 Mar. 1956.

hope that the outcome of labour administration might be more predictable than it had been in earlier years.[1]

The continuities with 1955 extended to the rules of administration as well as strategy. The drive towards total control of hiring was continued and by the time that the Labour Bureau Chiefs met to finalise the labour assignment plan in May 1956, it was claimed that all hiring was being administered by the Bureaux.[2]

In the event, the urban employment experience of 1956 confounded expectations, and although the final labour plan did allow for a substantial rise in employment, even this proved unrealistically small. For the expansion of urban employment was not only sufficient to absorb many unemployed, but also led to a reversal of participation trends. Increases in female labour and the absorption of many young, hitherto unemployed persons were particularly important. The increase in female participation was widely welcomed and taken as satisfaction of long unfulfilled promises such as those made at the time of the 1952 employment *decisions*;[3] and the absorption of younger persons into the labour force can be seen from the spectacular increases in apprentices. In Shanghai, for example, the number of apprentices absorbed in 1956 was more than twice the number absorbed in the previous five years.[4]

The work of the Labour Bureaux in this unexpected and somewhat exhilarating environment was very different from that envisaged only a few months earlier. In the first place control of hiring became impossible. This was partly because for most of the year the Bureaux staff were engrossed in wage reform work and partly because, as in 1951 and 1953, the volume of work and the pressures to allow free hiring were too great to make detailed control feasible. Thus whereas in May we found the Labour Bureaux Chiefs congratulating themselves on eliminating free hiring, by August the

[1] *CHCC* 1955 No. 9, especially pp. 3 and 13. Only relief and public security enterprises were exempted from the obligation to make labour plans.
[2] 'The national assignment plan for 1956 settled', *HWJP* 17 May 1956.
[3] 'Mobilise female strength and develop its activist value', *CFJP* 12 Aug. 1956; *CFJP* 18 Aug. 1956.
[4] 'The improvement in the welfare of the city's workers and staff', *CFJP* 28 Sep. 1956 and Chiang Meng-ch'iang and Kao Liu-wen, 'Some remaining problems in the increase of workers and staff in Shanghai industrial enterprises in 1956', *TCKT* 1957 No. 15, pp. 29–31.

Chief of the Shanghai Bureau was criticising the rigidity and inefficiency of the existing hiring procedures and agreeing to their relaxation.[1] The pressure for liberalisation continued up to the end of 1956 because labour administration became involved in the wider controversy of economic decentralisation. In this controversy, supporters of decentralisation argued that the efficiency of individual enterprises required local flexibility in the use of labour as well as capital, and at one point, in late 1956, the implications of decentralisation appeared so extreme that in some areas the labour planning organs were reported to be handing over their powers to local planning bodies and closing down.[2]

Another somersault in attitudes in 1956 was a new approach to migration. In early 1956, the outflow of population from Shanghai and other cities was continuing; part of this was to the rural areas and part was to the new, rapidly growing cities.[3] The return to the countryside was to some extent motivated by the propaganda and promises surrounding the cooperativisation campaign but many returned simply to protect their interests as best they might. Also, it has to be remembered that, prior to 1956, families had split their labour between rural and urban areas, with the men tending to work in the cities and the women remaining behind to do agricultural work or supervise rented property. After cooperativisation this was not tolerated. Rural cadres were under pressure to increase agricultural output and were therefore determined to maximise their supply of labour power – where necessary by resorting to intimidation. This was so effective that in Shanghai, on the eve of the urban leap forward, we find reports that the loss of workers to the countryside was causing some factories to shut down.[4]

[1] *CFJP* 12 Aug. 1956; 'The Labour Ministry holds a conference to decide on measures for solution of the problem of labour arrangement', *NCNA* 23 Apr. 1957 (*SCMP* 1521).

[2] 'Give enterprises appropriate powers of self-government', *HHPYK* 1956 No. 23, pp. 46–7. Chang Wan-chieh, 'Concerning the problem of the sphere of duties of the Provincial, Municipality and County Planning Committees' labour, wage and cadre training offices', *CHCC* 1956 No. 10, pp. 24–5.

[3] 'Implement overall planning, strengthen leadership policy and do labour assignment and hiring work well', *LT* 1956 No. 3, pp. 23–5; *KSJP* 14 Mar. 1956; *KSJP* 3 Mar. 1956.

[4] Cadres in Kiangsu were said to have addressed urban workers in these terms: 'you [who remain] in the factories affect agricultural output and must [therefore] immediately return home. If you do not [your families] will be treated as non-agricultural households

The outflow of labour to the key-point cities was a reflection of the policy of redistributing manpower resources on the lines laid down in the First Plan and in early 1956 the older cities, such as Shanghai, were not altogether unwilling to cooperate in this. One reason for this was that they were contending with an increase of unemployment which had resulted from the socialisation campaigns, particularly in commerce. But by the middle of the year, the problems of labour supply were so acute that we find the Shanghai Bureau, for example, bitterly regretting the contracts by which labour transfers had taken place.[1] This situation seems to have been widespread in urban China in summer 1956, as the demands of construction, transport and industry for labour mounted and rural cadres continued to recruit in the urban areas.

As a result of all this we find the Labour Ministry having to take measures to ensure that urban labour needs were met, and the Shanghai Bureau trying to renegotiate some of its inter-city and Provincial labour contracts.[2] This latter was however no easy task, even though the workers involved were themselves very anxious to return to Shanghai. In the case of one big contract with the Province of Shensi, the best that the Shanghai Bureau could manage was an agreement that in the first instance it would attempt to recruit from workers sent back to the Kiangsu countryside in the 1955 *hsia fang*, and that if it could not meet its requirements in this way, it could request the return of workers from Shensi.

Autumn 1956: The return from the countryside

By late 1956 the exceptional factors that had led to net emigration from Shanghai in 1955 and early 1956 had spent their force. The harvest of 1956 was below expectations and the curtailment of subsidiary activities accentuated the impact of this on incomes. This setback was due to natural factors and mismanagement, and also

and their land will be divided again and given to others and [they will receive] no further supply of grain'; 'Do not force workers to return to rural areas', *JMJP* 19 Apr. 1956.

[1] *CFJP* 11 Aug. 1956.

[2] 'Strengthen labour force assignment work', *LT* 1956 No. 8, pp. 30–2; 'Agricultural cooperatives must organise manpower to help industrial construction', *JMJP* 9 Jun. 1956; 'Mobilise Shanghai workers to settle down to participating in construction in Shensi', *SHJP* 9 Sep. 1956.

to the disincentive effect resulting from the fact that members of the new cooperatives were worked very hard.[1] We do not know of any out-turn figures for this, but the 1956 agricultural plan for the Shanghai suburbs estimated that the number of working days per household would be 259; which may be compared with 210 in 1955 and a figure of 100 that was mentioned for the pre-collectivisation period.[2] If this sort of increase did occur (and the technical reforms attempted and the water and conservation work claimed to have been done suggest that they did) then it cannot be surprising that there were many migrants like those returning to Canton in autumn 1956, who were reported as saying, 'anything is better than this'.[3]

In addition to the return of recently '*hsia fanged*' urban residents and peasants, there was also a substantial inflow of families of urban workers and staff who had remained in the countryside. These families often owned land and housing in the rural areas, and when the cooperatives were set up they had the choice of persuading their urban relations to return, or of moving themselves into the cities. They could not remain in the countryside since the collectives' income distribution policy – based on the principle that income was to be dependent on work – implied a drastic reduction in their living standards. As 1956 progressed, increasing numbers of people in this position opted for total removal to the cities.[4]

1957: THE MAKING OF A NEW EMPLOYMENT STRATEGY

In attempting to reconstruct Chinese economic policy in the 1950s, one has constantly to avoid the temptation of linking together policy statements and administrative measures to give them an appearance of design and coherence that exaggerates the degree to which, in reality, they comprised an articulate and fully comprehended plan.

[1] 'Struggle to enable the great majority of cooperative members to increase their incomes', *HWJP* 23 Nov. 1956; 'Rationally solve the unemployment problem', *Che ch'iang jih pao* 7 May 1957; 'Do agricultural production work well in the suburbs [of Shanghai] so that it is appropriate to the needs of the city's industrial production', *CFJP* 12 Aug. 1956.
[2] 'Fully use agricultural manpower', *WHP* 21 Mar. 1956.
[3] *Tzu yu chen hsien* (The free battle front), (Hong Kong) 17 Sep. 1956.
[4] A very good account of this process is 'After increasing output it will be possible to raise the people's standard of living', *LNJP* 24 Dec. 1956.

This is particularly the case in 1957. For this was a formative year during which the principles of economic policy were uncertain and the subject of acute controversy. But although this was so, we think it possible to trace the development of a new strategy for employment which had its origins in late 1956, and its culmination in early 1958. And even if in the first instance this strategy was not fully worked out, the logical and practical interdependence of its different aspects justifies our considering it as a whole.

The employment plan for 1957

The loss of hiring control in 1956 had led to an increase in employment that almost fulfilled the plan for the whole of the First Five Year Plan period and since the 1957 plans for output were very conservative, the demand for labour from the public sector was bound to be small. This was confirmed in April, when the annual Labour Assignment Conference issued a gloomy communiqué which stated that the 1956 labour intake had been in excess of 1957 requirements, and which reflected widespread fears of redundancy – particularly in construction.[1]

In July, Po I-po announced the official plan figures and these showed that although average employment of workers and staff in 1957 was expected to be 4·7% higher than the 1956 level, total employment at the end of 1957 would be marginally lower than the peak reached at the end of 1956.[2]

This prospect of stagnant demand for labour has to be matched with certain special aspects of the labour supply situation in 1957. For in addition to the natural increment to the labour force there were three other elements in the supply of labour in that year: the renewed flow of migrants seeking jobs;[3] a net outflow of manpower from the army;[4] and a sharp reduction in the intake of young people into the educational system.

[1] *HWJP* 24 Apr. 1957.
[2] Po I-po, 'Report on the out-turn of the 1956 national economic plan and the draft plan for 1957', *HHPYK* 1957 No. 14, pp. 28–39.
[3] 700,000 flowed into Shanghai between June 1956 and September 1957, *WHP* 7 Aug. 1958.
[4] 'This year's number of demobilised soldiers is much greater than the number of new soldiers', *HWJP* 5 Apr. 1957.

We noted the significance of the growth of the educational system in our discussion of Shanghai's labour supply and we showed how rapid changes in the growth of the educational retention had had a favourable effect on the problem of employment absorption. But this effect could only continue until the limits to educational expansion imposed by cost and the supply of suitable urban employment began to take effect. This happened in 1957, and as a result there was a sharp drop in the rate of growth of the intake into the middle schools and an absolute decline in university entry. The effect of this was to sharpen the educational pyramid and to reduce the net off-take from the labour market. The decline in university entrants meant that for the first time since 1953 the intake into the universities was less than the number of graduates from the Senior Middle Schools.

The outcome is illustrated in Diagram 5. This shows the inflow and outflow from the Higher Middle Schools from 1953 to 1957 (the size of the net inflow being indicated by the gap between the two lines). The dotted lines show what could be expected up to 1960 on the assumption that the inflow remained at the 1957 level. It will be seen that in 1959 there was the prospect of a large net outflow, and thereafter the net outflow would be nil. 1957, therefore, was the beginning of a serious crisis in the educational system which had important educational and political repercussions as well as implications for employment.[1]

Employment and the second five year plan

The new status given to employment questions in 1957 rested on more than short-term considerations. For reflection on the employment experience of the First Five Year and tentative calculations of the employment implications of the Second and Third Plans, brought home to the Government the structural nature of the problem. At the national level, Sung P'ing, Li Fu-ch'un and numerous others demonstrated that since the maximum proposed increase in employ-

[1] The authoritative account of this crisis is a speech by Chang Hsi-jo (Minister of Education), 'Concerning the employment problems of Junior and Middle school students who cannot continue their education and the school starting age', *CFJP* 17 Mar. 1957. See also, 'This year's higher education intake is 107,000', *CFJP* 27 Mar. 1957.

ment during the Second Plan was 7 million jobs, a cumulative increase of unemployment in the whole economy of upwards of 5 million a year could be expected.[1]

Perspective calculations were also made at the local level and all

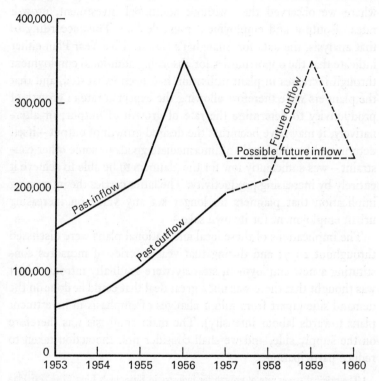

5. Inflow and outflow from the Higher Middle School system: the situation in 1957.
Source: p. 35, n. l.

cities were required to incorporate plans for the elimination of unemployment in their overall plans for 1957-62. In Shanghai, the proposed rate of growth of industry in the Second Plan was 9·7% per annum (compared with an out-turn of 14% in the First Plan). But whereas in the First Plan there had been a net labour input of

[1] 'Develop research into the population problem', *WHP* 21 Feb. 1957 and 'Birth control and my country's population problem', *WHP* 16 Mar. 1957. Sung P'ing *HH* 1957 No. 12, pp. 25-8.

260,000, in the Second, the net planned increase of employment in industry was to be negligible.[1] Taken in conjunction with the planned *reduction* in the size of the bureaucracy, this implied that prospects for net growth of total employment in the modern sector were nil. This confirms our earlier analysis of Shanghai growth, where we observed that, without additional investment, growth rates of output and employment must decline. Thus according to that analysis, the data for Shanghai's Second Five Year Plan either indicate that the opportunities for absorbing additional employment through increases in plant utilisation had been exhausted, and that the planners were therefore allowing the expected rate of growth of productivity to determine the rate of growth of output; or alternatively, it may have been that the desired growth of output – itself determined by the supply of intermediate goods or some other constraint – was sufficiently low for the planners to be able to achieve it entirely by increasing productivity. The latter carries the interesting implication that planners no longer set any value on increasing urban employment for its own sake.[2]

The implications of these local and national plans were discussed throughout 1957; and during that year a series of measures constituting a new employment strategy were gradually introduced. It was thought that there was not a great deal that could be done on the demand side (apart from minor changes of emphasis in investment plans towards labour intensity). The main emphasis was therefore on the supply side, and we shall consider first the action taken to reduce participation.

[1] The original target rate of growth for industry in Shanghai's First Five Year Plan was 11·1% per annum. The Plan was reported as fulfilled in September 1956 and the final out-turn represented a growth rate of 14·1%; 'A marked increase in Shanghai's industrial and agricultural output', *WHP* 5 Jan. 1957. 'Shanghai industry contributes one fifth', *HWJP* 30 Sep. 1957. Targets implying rates of 9·7% and 8·3% were announced in August 1956 for the Second and Third Plans. See, *HWJP* 8 Aug. 1956. The labour plan for the Second and Third Plans are in *CFJP* 11 Aug. 1956. It should be noted that the Second and Third Plan targets vary slightly in different texts. This is presumably due to the fact that the planners were perpetually recalculating on the basis of changing out-turns of current plans. The differences however are not significant.

[2] Perspective calculations revealed that even some key-point areas were faced with serious absorption problems. In Kirin Province, for example, it was reported that the annual natural increase of the province's population in the late 1950s was 300,000. This was compared with a total increase in the numbers of workers and staff between 1949 and 1957 of 500,000, *CLJP* 14 Aug. 1957.

Participation rates

We have already seen how control of participation was used after 1952 to minimise open unemployment. In 1956, however, participation limits were widely relaxed and high expectations of future possibilities for participation were aroused. The problem in 1957 therefore was to reverse this; having already almost completely exhausted the possibilities of reducing participation by eliminating child labour and reducing hours.

The first objective was renewed limitation of female participation. The difficulty here was that no legal limitation was possible and recourse therefore had to be made to propaganda campaigns that emphasised that domestic work was as real a contribution to economic construction as work in a factory. From the speed with which this campaign was reversed in 1958, it would seem that it met little enthusiasm.[1]

Another form of participation limitation introduced in 1957 was a lengthening of the apprenticeship period. Together with other changes in apprentice arrangements, this change, while not limiting participation in work, did have the effect of slowing down the automatic element in the growth of the permanent work force which previously had been related to the very short apprentice times served.[2]

The most important aspect of participation control in this period was a further reform of the retirement regulations. It will be recalled that there had been a crisis in 1955 over this, and that in that year new regulations were introduced to govern retirement from state administrative and similar organs. Despite this reform, it was reported that up to 1956 only 62,000 persons had actually retired from enterprises and only 1,000 from state administrative organs. An effort was made therefore to correct the defects in the old regulations in a new set published in November 1957.[3]

[1] 'The problem of female employment can only be solved gradually', *CFJP* 13 Dec. 1956. See also, *Chü'an kuo chih kung chia shu tai piao hui i chu yao wen chien* (Important documents from the national conference of dependants of workers and staff), (1957).

[2] *State Council Communication on lengthening the apprentice time limit, HHPYK* 1957 No. 11, p. 121. An important People's Daily editorial on the subject is reported in *HHPYK* 1957 No. 12, pp. 123–4.

[3] *State Council draft regulations on the management of retirement of workers and staff,*

The effect of these regulations was to ensure that formal retirement provisions, which previously had been legally applicable only in a minority of enterprises and organisations, were implemented throughout the whole of the modern sector. The regulations also removed what were in effect bonus payments to persons who stayed on in employment after retirement age.

The population plans for the second five year plan

Although control of total population was only a long-term solution to employment problems, it undoubtedly received more publicity than any other aspect of the labour supply question. The relationship between population and employment was not a new topic for discussion. In 1953, population control had been rejected on the grounds that the First Plan would generate sufficient employment to utilise a large and rapidly growing population. In 1954, the idea of control came back into favour and it is possible – but not certain – that this may have reflected current employment difficulties as well as a new recognition of the food problem.[1] In 1956 there was further debate on the question but predictably enough, we find on the whole that the optimism engendered by the rapid growth of employment was reflected in rejection of population control programmes which, it was argued, had been rendered obsolete by the arrival of socialism.[2]

In 1957 the advocates of population control came into their own again. In the early part of the year the press devoted considerable space to the problem and special population conferences were held by the Health, Labour and other interested Ministries.[3] The debate

---

HHPYK 1957 No. 24, pp. 89–91. This regulation cancelled the 1951, 1953 and 1955 retirement regulations. In 1956 it was admitted that in the coal industry alone, nearly 7% of the workforce was due for retirement. Sung Shao-wen, 'Labour balancing and assignment work in the Great Leap Forward', *CHCC* 1958 No. 4, p. 4.

[1] 'A criticism of reactionary, modern Chinese population theories', *HCS* 1955 No. 12.

[2] 'Unemployment disappearing in China', *TKP* (Hong Kong) 16 Oct. 1956. Also 'Chu Te's speech', *CFJP* 19 Sep. 1956. But opinion was not unanimous in 1956; for a contrary view see, 'For the active dissemination of contraceptive knowledge', *KMJP* 3 Aug. 1956 (*SCMP* 1352).

[3] At least one theorist argued that employment should be the first criterion in considering the optimum size of population; 'A discussion of optimum population size', *WHP* 27 Apr. 1957. At the Labour Ministry conference speakers included Chen Ta and Fei Hsiao-t'ung, 'Research on the problems of China's population', *Che ch'iang jih pao* 16 Mar. 1957.

was closely related to current employment issues, and was climaxed and concluded in February when Mao made his speech, *On the correct handling of contradictions among the people*. We do not have the original text of this speech, but it was followed six days later by a People's Daily editorial advocating birth control and an article in the Shanghai press on 14 March states unequivocally that this policy had been advocated by Chairman Mao in his speech.[1]

At the city level, population plans involved action both on vital rates and control over population movement, and as with employment, cities made plans for population growth consistent with their Second Five Year Plan.

In Shanghai, the first population plan was discussed in January 1957, but the final plan was not announced until January 1958 – when it reflected the urgency of the problems created by the renewed population inflow of 1957. Basically the plan envisaged that the population should be stabilised at 7 millions and this was to be achieved by emigration and a reduction of the natural growth rate from 3·3% to 1·3%.[2]

It is an extraordinary reflection of the continuity in Shanghai planning that the figure of 7 millions was first put forward as a maximum population for Shanghai in a report published in 1946 – at a time when the city's population was only 4 millions.[3] It would seem that this early estimate must have been based on a perceptive analysis of maximum future population density and possible configurations of land use, for we know that later on in 1958 the planners were arguing that if there was any population growth in excess of 7 millions, this would have to take place in self-sufficient satellite cities rather than within the existing built up area.[4]

[1] 'Exercise appropriate birth control', *JMJP* 5 Mar. 1957 (*SCMP* 1487), and *WHP* 14 Mar. 1957.
[2] This was to be achieved by a combination of contraception and late marriage. Based on 'Mobilise surplus urban labour power; help socialist agricultural construction', *WHP* 7 Jan. 1958; 'Reduce the natural population growth rate of Shanghai to 2%', *WHP* 23 Jan. 1958; *NCNA* 9 Sep. 1957 (*SCMP* 1608).
[3] *Ta Shang hai tu shih chi hua ts'ung t'u ch'u k'ao pao kao shu* (Report on the preliminary outline plan for Greater Shanghai), (1946). This survey analysed the prospects for the development of the whole of the Shanghai area in the period following the defeat of the Japanese.
[4] 'Problems in the planning of satellite towns around Shanghai', *Chien chu hsüeh pao* (Architectural study journal), 1956 No. 8.

On the employment side, the population plan envisaged that there would be 500,000 new entrants to the labour force, but since there was to be a negligible net increase in industrial employment only 100,000 of these could be employed in the city's industry as replacements for anticipated retirements.

It can be seen that these proposals had important implications for emigration and the details of the Shanghai plan suggest that during the five year period of the Second Plan there would have to be emigration of about 1 million persons, of whom 40% would be of working age.

This type of population stabilisation could, of course, only be achieved in selected areas; but it is interesting that the idea of a long-term programme to stabilise China's total population also had some currency at this time. Li Fu-ch'un, for example, envisaged a fifteen year tapering-off period after which population would remain constant at 700 millions. That these ideas emanated from such highly placed persons shows the extent to which in 1957 the anti-Malthusian population expansionism of the early years of the First Plan had been routed.[1]

The 'hsia fang' movement

The employment and population plans for 1957 required a renewal of the effort to reverse the rural–urban migration. This is generally known as the *hsia fang* movement and in 1957 this movement reflected final recognition that the process of rural–urban population transfer would have to be postponed for a generation, and that Chinese economic strategy constituted a break with the socialist pattern of development as exemplified by the Soviet Union and Eastern Europe. As Wang Kuang-wei wrote in his classic article of August 1957, 'in this respect we differ from fraternal socialist countries'.[2]

Although the *hsia fang* movement can be fitted into the general revision of employment strategy, it is worth noting that in its origins it was also a series of separate movements which in the course of

[1] *WHP* 14. Mar. 1957.
[2] Wang Kuang-wei, 'Views on the arrangement of the agricultural labour force', *CHCC* 1957 No. 8, pp. 6–9.

the year gradually coalesced into a single, massive, population out-flow. In the first place, it was one of the long series of drives to return migrant peasants to the countryside, starting as usual in time for the spring planting.[1] Secondly it was related to the drive to eliminate bureaucracy and overmanning. In Shanghai this move-ment started in late 1956 and it continued on a national scale right up to the end of 1957. In the early stages, being 'sent down' did not necessarily mean being sent to the countryside – it usually implied being transferred from administrative or office work to participate in practical or physical work in schools, on the shop floors, etc. Thus an important aspect of this was the attempt to persuade cadres to work in small-scale enterprises where the potential for increased labour intensive production was considerable, but unutilised for lack of competent management.[2] As time passed, however, the cadre *hsia fang* movement became increasingly a movement to transfer cadres to the rural areas where lack of administrative resources was endangering the collectivisation movement and a complete re-organisation of local government was taking place.

A third component of the *hsia fang* was the campaign to solve the problem of student unemployment. For in 1957 there was no satis-factory urban solution to this. The students therefore had to join the exodus to the rural areas where it was hoped that some of their skills would be of value. In order to facilitate this transfer the revised version of the Twelve Year Plan for Agricultural Development pro-vided for the absorption of unemployed students, and by November the People's Daily reported that 2 million Middle and Junior school graduates had left the cities for rural work.[3]

Finally, the *hsia fang* was also the return to the countryside of the families of workers and staff who had migrated into the towns in

[1] 'Shanghai mobilises peasants to return to the countryside', *WHP* 14 Mar. 1957.

[2] 'Simplification of the structure must be combined with reform of the system', *HHPYK* 1957 No. 6, pp. 14–15; 'Four hundred Shanghai administrative cadres transfer to work at the basic level', *CHJP* 21 Jan. 1957 and 'Go to the small factory', *CFJP* 12 Apr. 1957. A very interesting example of the sort of analysis which was undertaken in the 'simplification' campaign is, 'See the necessity for simplification in the grain ministry from statistical data', *TCKT* 1957 No. 8, pp. 9–12.

[3] See the sections on education in *HHPYK* 1957 Nos. 7, 9 and 16. The revised Agricultural Plan is in *HHPYK* 1957 No. 22 and the relevant section is on p. 128; 'Must establish home and work in the countryside', People's Daily editorial, *HHPYK* 1957 No. 23, pp. 165–7.

search of higher living standards. A survey published in July 1957 showed that in fifteen major cities, 60% of the population were classified as non-productive and that the rate of growth of this section of the urban population was higher than that of the 'productives'.[1] It was this group that put severe pressure on urban food and housing supply, and unless its growth could be controlled the Government would be forced to make a reallocation of resources that would undermine the investment strategy of the Second Plan. In order to facilitate the return of families and make enforced separation more humane, the Government introduced new measures which were to enable workers to visit their families on a regular basis.[2]

These then were the tributaries that merged in late 1957 and early 1958 into a large-scale population flow from the towns. Overall it was a remarkable achievement. About 1 million people were moved (apart from the students) compared with 800,000 in the *hsia fang* of 1955. For the most part they were moved without force although the movement was related to a rectification campaign of considerable vigour.[3] In one respect, however, the 1957 *hsia fang* differed from its predecessors; this was in the explicit recognition that underlying the campaign was the power and right of the authorities responsible for employment and population to assign individuals to their places of residence and work. In our next section we shall consider the way in which this principle affected the work of the Labour Bureaux.

THE LABOUR BUREAUX REFORM THEIR WORK; THE ENLARGEMENT OF THE SPHERE OF ASSIGNMENT

The attention given to labour and population issues in 1957 gave new stature to the Labour Bureaux and a new lease of life to their

---

[1] 'The non-productive population of the cities is too large and growing too fast', *NCNA* 25 Jul. 1957.

[2] 'Workers and staff must persuade their families to return to the countryside', *HWJP* 10 Apr. 1957. The regulations on holiday visiting are in *HHPYK* 1957 No. 24, p. 95. Separation of families in this way was a well known pre-war phenomenon, notably in Manchuria, Dugald Christie, *Thirty years in Moukden: 1883-1913* (1914), p. 17.

[3] The directive on rectification was reported in Shanghai on 1 May; this was followed on 15 May by the directive on cadre participation in physical labour which was a key element in the *hsia fang* campaign. *HWJP* 1 May 1957, *HWJP* 15 May 1957.

activities. This was much needed, since in 1956 there were signs that labour administration at the local level was disintegrating. By early 1957, however, it was apparent that the new employment policies, both tactical and strategic, required that the duties of the Bureaux be multiplied rather than diminished. And in the course of 1957, it became clear that fulfilment of the employment plan and the *hsia fang* campaign both required that the sphere of hiring control be increased.[1] To some extent control was automatically increased because by the end of 1957 many centrally controlled enterprises had been handed over to local authorities and therefore fell within local labour plans. In addition to organisational change, however, what is important is that whereas in 1952 and 1955 the demand for control was an unheeded byproduct of the Bureaux' problems, in 1957 control was recognised as a primary object of policy and given a new and potent theoretical foundation by Chairman Mao in his speech on 'Contradictions'. The relevant passage is as follows:

'In drawing up plans, handling affairs or thinking over problems, we must proceed from the fact that China has a population of six hundred million people. This must never be forgotten.

'Now why should we make a point of this? Could it be that there are people who still do not know that we have a population of six hundred million? Of course everyone knows this, but in actual practice some are apt to forget it and act as if they thought that the fewer people and the smaller their world the better ... I hope these people will take a wider view and really recognize the fact that we have a population of six hundred million, that this is an objective fact, and that this is our asset ... Our guiding principle (in resolving the contradictions inherent in a large population), is overall planning and all round consideration, and proper arrangements. No matter whether it is a question of food, natural calamities, employment, education, the intellectuals, the United Front of all Patriotic Forces, the National Minorities, or any other question we must always proceed from the standpoint of overall planning and all round consideration for the whole people.'

The impact of this speech on the Labour Bureaux' work was immediate, and throughout the year its key phrases were used to

---

[1] *LT* 1957 No. 3, pp. 2-3; *LT* 1957 11 and 12 *passim*.

justify compulsory assignment of school and university graduates, temporary construction workers, excess manpower in industrial and administrative units, and the non-productive dependents of workers and staff.[1] Control of these groups was not easily obtained; students were particularly vociferous but other groups also tried to resist undesirable assignment with appeals to their freedoms written into the Constitution and adherence to what became known as 'The Five Won't Do's'.[2]

The control of university graduates was not primarily a Labour Bureau responsibility, but it is interesting to see the way in which the handling of assignment in this sphere ran parallel to the new trends in ordinary Labour Bureau work. Assignment of graduates had started in 1950 and in theory had continued down to 1957.[3] But in practice control of graduates was not easy, particularly as in 1956, when demand for graduates was reported as being three times as great as supply.[4] In 1957, graduate assignment became an important issue in the Hundred Flowers Campaign in which rightists were reported to be demanding a 'free market for ability'.[5] It became necessary, therefore, to make further efforts to obtain voluntary submission to official assignment plans – and this was done in 1957 by reinforcing the official plan with the sanction that graduates who refused assignments would not be offered a second chance, while enterprises or state organs that accepted officially assigned graduates were forbidden absolutely to hire 'free' graduates looking for employment.[6]

[1] For example in November the People's Daily published a very important editorial on labour matters entitled, 'Proceed from 600 million', *HHPYK* 1958 No. 1, pp. 41–3.

[2] The five were: (1) 'Leave Peking – will not do'; (2) 'Not able to go home every day – will not do'; (3) 'Repetitious work – will not do'; (4) 'Dirty work – will not do'; and (5) 'Pay low – will not do'. See, 'Thought problems in employment work must be overcome', *TKP* (Peking) 25 Sep. 1957.

[3] For 1950 assignment see, *JMJP* 23 Jul. 1950. A vivid personal account of graduate assignment in this early period is Maria Yen, *The umbrella garden* (1954).

[4] Some revealing stories appear in *Tao kuo chia hsü yao wo ti ti fang ch'ü* (To the place where the fatherland needs us), (1956). There is a striking picture in the Peking Museum of Post Revolution Art which shows a group of young people working in the mountains. The picture has the same title as the book mentioned above and is dated 1956. For data on the demand and supply of graduates in 1956 and a fascinating survey of assignment experience in earlier years see, 'Contradiction between the supply and demand for university graduates', *CFJP* 2 Jun. 1957

[5] 'University graduates determine to submit to planned distribution', *HWJP* 27 Jul. 1957.

[6] *Some decisions of principle concerning the work of distributing university graduates in summer 1957*, *HHPYK* 1957 No. 16, pp. 203–4.

Population movement control and labour controls

Control of rural–urban manpower movements continued to be an important aspect of the Bureaux' hiring control work in 1957 and temporary recruitment of rural labour was put onto a more reliable basis, not only to guarantee the adequacy of supply, but also to ensure that the construction industry did not again become the means of illicit population transfer. For although new *hu k'ou* regulations were introduced in late 1957, the experience of the 1950s showed that such regulations needed the support of effective labour market controls. The upshot of this was the introduction of a new system whereby temporary labour transfers were governed by collective contracts between the agricultural cooperatives and the hiring units, the terms of such contracts being subject to Labour Bureau approval.[1]

The administration of unemployment

Although the gravity of the urban unemployment crisis was leading to a radical new emphasis on the absorptive capacity of agriculture, even this could not offer an immediate and completely satisfactory solution to the problem, and throughout 1957 unemployment of different kinds lingered on in the cities. In many areas the machinery for administering relief had been completely dismantled by the end of 1956 and although it was not formally rehabilitated in 1957 something had to be done. One reason for this was that unemployment became an issue in the Hundred Flowers Campaign and the Rectification Campaign, and the authorities were anxious to demonstrate the truth of their frequently repeated assertion that unemployment was a phenomenon associated only with capitalist economies.[2] The difficulty was that budgetary retrenchment and the abandonment of the unemployment levy left only minimal funds for unemployment relief. In these circumstances the Bureaux had to

---

[1] *State Council temporary regulations concerning the hiring by units of temporary workers from the countryside, JMJP* 14 Dec. 1957.

[2] 'The cry of one who is unemployed', *KJJP* 16 May 1957; 'The Labour Bureau conscientiously deals with the views of representatives of the People's Congress', *CFJP* 3 Aug. 1957.

fall back on the policy of encouraging the development of small enterprises to which they sometimes contributed a small quantity of working capital. There is evidence that the Bureaux found the organisation of such units very difficult and that cadres preferred relief work to take the form of simple cash or grain hand-outs. However, after pressure had been brought to bear in the Rectification campaign, relief production units were started up on a wide scale.[1]

The viability of relief units required that they be granted a certain degree of freedom both in factor and product markets, and it is this that links the unemployment problem of 1957 with the Government's decision to re-open the free market in the urban areas for specified categories of goods, and also with the partial relaxation of the hiring controls.[2] The relationship between the free market and unemployment was explicitly recognised, as one municipal level spokesman put it: 'the opening of the free market [leads to] many new opportunities for self-found employment'.

It is only in the light of these aspects of unemployment work that one can appreciate the full irony of the dilemma facing the Government in its handling of illicit 'autonomous' enterprises. For we saw in Chapter 1 how the Government was divided between desire to eliminate the autonomous enterprises and the need to tolerate them for employment reasons. But from the practical point of view there was no possible distinction between autonomous enterprises and relief units. Both were capable of rapid growth from small beginnings and both could frustrate plans in the public sector; the only difference was that one was regarded as illicit capitalism and the other was a licit creation of the Labour Bureaux.[3] It would therefore have been absurd to eliminate the one and tolerate the other.

[1] 'The Labour Bureau reforms its work', *HWJP* 3 Aug. 1957; *CFJP* 3 Aug. 1957; 'Can urban unemployment be solved', *CKCNP* 16 Jul. 1957; 'Organise relief production units', *CCJP* 9 Oct. 1957.

[2] See the Shenyang Labour Bureau Report for 1957, *SYJP* 2 Aug. 1957; 'Many methods of solving the unemployment problem', *Che ch'iang jih pao* 14 May 1957, 'How many apprentices can handicraft and service trades hire?' *LT* 1957 No. 16, pp. 14–15.

[3] Average employment in relief units up to the end of 1955 was thirteen persons, see, *NCNA* 4 Feb. 1955. However, the classic example of a relief unit that made good – *The Shanghai Iron Bed Vehicle Accessory Cooperative* – grew from 3 to 199 persons in four years; 'Business has endlessly enlarged in the three years from the establishment of the cooperative', *HWJP* 11 Apr. 1954.

This was the Achilles heel of the new employment strategy as it emerged in 1957. For this strategy required full control of the urban labour market, and although the Bureaux succeeded in enlarging the sphere of their control over hiring, as long as small-scale enterprises were allowed to flourish and hire freely, control could never be absolute. The existence of a free sector of the labour market was bound to undermine the ultimate sanction against those who resisted assignment – the threat that they would remain unemployed indefinitely – and bound also to make control of rural–urban migration difficult. By the end of 1957 this was understood, and in mid-1958 it was reported that in Shanghai the autonomous enterprises had been eliminated.[1] The last spark of capitalism had been extinguished in the flood of the Great Leap Forward and the Labour Bureaux were, at least for a moment, in full control.

[1] 'Caution needed in absorbing autonomous enterprises', *HWJP* 20 Apr. 1958.

8

THE AFTERMATH OF CENTRAL PLANNING

Conclusions of two kinds may be drawn from this study: those relating to labour market organisation, and those relating to wider issues of development strategy in China's First and Second Five Year Plans.

The most striking change in labour market organisation in the late 1950s was the development of comprehensive powers over urban hiring through a decentralisation of administration. It is vital for us to understand why control of hiring became such a serious issue and why decentralisation was thought necessary to accomplish this. We think that the case can be summarised as follows.

THE CASE FOR HIRING CONTROL

(1) The First Five Year Plan was built around a core of projects which were to constitute a small but coherent base for future industrial growth, and the labour supply for these had to be guaranteed. This was not easy. Priority work was frequently in remote and harsh locations and labour in other cities strongly resisted inducements to redeployment. This was partly because transfer often resulted in loss of real income and because migrant labour was sometimes discriminated against in key-point areas with respect to housing, rations, etc. Moreover, there is evidence that even unemployed workers preferred to remain in familiar urban areas, subsisting on resources supplied by casual or illicit work, rather than move to assured employment elsewhere. This suggests that labour immobility also had its roots in values and preferences unrelated to, and at times in conflict with, what would seem economically rational.

In the mid-1950s, the labour planners attempted to solve this problem by a system that combined limited direct controls to satisfy key-point requirements, with a comparatively liberal system elsewhere. But this mixed system proved difficult to sustain, since those subject to control could usually escape into the 'free sector'. The conclusion was therefore that control of part of the urban labour force required control of the whole.

(2) Structural trends in urban employment – even allowing for reduction in the natural growth rate of the urban population – implied that to keep a reasonable proportion of the population of working age in employment in some of the older cities, there would have to be continuous out-migration. Experience showed, that without control of hiring, the difficulties of securing this were formidable. For although the urban authorities had a wide range of sanctions and inducements that they could use to encourage emigration, the power to ensure that those who resisted were deprived of all possible employment opportunities was recognised as indispensible.

(3) The urban overhead costs of industrial growth had proved higher than expected, and this meant that future urban population growth had to be minimised as far as was consistent with the planned rate of industrialisation.[1] One corollary of this was that the demand for labour from expanding enterprises and sectors should be met by the supply of labour released by productivity growth in the modern sector, mechanisation in the traditional sector and controlled increases in participation.[2] Given the inertia, the tendency to bureaucratic employment expansion and the weakness of financial controls evident in the 1950s, it seems probable that these intra-city transfers could only be accomplished by the intervention of an agency external to the enterprises and units involved.

(4) The traditional sector had employment functions that required external employment control. In the short run, the planned reduction of urban population was not sufficient to eliminate unemployment; and because of the constraints on expansion in the public sector, the traditional sector was left with an important role in employment *absorption*. Thus the immediate problem was to maximise traditional employment subject to the constraints of

[1] Christopher Howe, 'The supply and administration of urban housing in mainland China: the case of Shanghai', *China Quarterly* January–March 1968, pp. 73–97.

[2] 'The age structure of urban residents and urban development plans', *CSCS* 1957 No. 3, p. 5.

current participation policies, the plans for overall urban population growth, and the supply of non-labour inputs.

In the longer run, however, as argued in (3), the function of the traditional sector was to supply labour to the modern sector, and this required the execution of a carefully controlled programme of *disabsorption*. Both these functions of the traditional sector necessitated direct intervention in the labour market.

(5) In the First Plan there had been some attempt to use the structure of wages as an instrument for securing the desired allocation of the labour force as between industries, areas and occupations. And it is significant that 1956, the year of the most comprehensive planned reform of the wage structure, was also the year in which direct hiring controls were most widely abandoned. By 1957, however, it was appreciated that structural wage reform was more difficult than had been expected and that it was in any case a costly and inefficient device.[1] Particularly important was the fact that structural wage reform kept pushing up the average and total wage bill to the extent that it was seriously limiting the use of resources for investment, and creating incentives for rural–urban migration.[2] The alternative to further manipulation of the wage structure was to allocate labour directly.

The use of direct controls left some major problems in securing efficient utilisation of the labour force unsolved. But in the absence of techniques for quantifying the losses involved the case for substituting administrative for wage controls must have appeared strong.

As a result of considerations such as these, we find that control of hiring – first mooted as a byproduct of unemployment administration in 1950 and later extended to select groups such as graduates and construction workers – became a major object of labour administration.[3] Next, we have to consider why efficient control was seen to require decentralisation.

---

[1] For a discussion of this see, Christopher Howe, 'Wage structure and wage policy in Chinese industry', in Janet G. Chapman and Shun-hsin Chou, editors, *The economies of the Communist world*, (forthcoming, 1971).

[2] Between 1952 and 1957, money wages of workers and staff rose by 47·1%, *Ten great years*, p. 216.

[3] A number of major cities had implemented labour control regulations during the Anti-Japanese war. These regulations were designed to stop labour pilfering and stipu-

THE CASE FOR DECENTRALISATION

(1) The decentralisation of labour administration that started in 1957 was part of a wider movement that gave substantial economic planning powers to the provincial and municipal levels of government. To some extent this reform was a consequence of the urban socialisation, since this had brought into the public sector thousands of small scale enterprises. Many of these enterprises were subject to seasonal fluctuation and their control required knowledge and flexibility that could only be supplied at the local level. At the same time, it was also argued that local planning under Party leadership would facilitate more effective mobilisation of resources than had been possible under a bureaucratic, centralised system.[1] In administrative terms, the creation of decentralised clusters of decision-making groups, working within broad policy lines, could be expected to minimise communication costs and in other ways economise the use of administrative resources.

(2) Apart from these general considerations, the case for decentralisation of employment planning was particularly strong, since under the old system responsibility for labour control had been diffused among a variety of organisations whose interests in local labour markets were frequently competitive, and whose activities were not subject to effective coordination. As a result, the Labour Ministry was unable to build up the network of control and information channels necessary for meaningful employment planning. When such planning was seen to be essential, reform followed. Even after reform, however, local plans remained subject to central (Labour Ministry) allocation work. But there were no rules for reconciling local and central plans and the growing authority of local coordination is unmistakable.[2]

lated that no factory should employ persons already in employment in another factory. See, *China handbook: 1943* (1943), pp. 469–70.

[1] *State Council resolution on the reform of the system of industrial management*, *HHPYK* 1957 No. 24, pp. 57–9: Wang Kuei-wu, 'A great reform in the method of drawing up annual plans', *CHCC* 1958 No. 9, pp. 13–15; Schurmann, ch. IV; *CFJP* 11 Aug. 1956.

[2] The 1958 directive on the reform of the planning system left local–central relations vague. For 1959, however, primacy of local plans and balancing was made clear. *Chung Hua jen min kung ho kuo fa kuei hui pien* No. 8 July–Dec. 1958 pp. 96–9. Wang Kuei-wu, as cited above. The best general account of this reform is Audrey Donnithorne, *China's economic system* (1967) ch. 17.

It was logical that reform should unify hiring powers and give them to organisations whose territorial control span was approximately coterminous with effective local labour markets – that is areas within which it was possible to change employment without a permanent change of residence. After the imposition of draconian controls over internal migration in early 1958, the effective labour market was the municipality, together with the rural suburbs directly governed by it.[1] The expansion of municipality jurisdiction, which in the case of important cities such as Shanghai greatly extended their power over adjacent rural areas, probably meant that in some cases the effective local labour market did not do too much violence to the 'natural' labour market – if we define the latter as the area within which employment mobility would have been common in the absence of artificial restrictions on movement.[2] And there is evidence that the planners were aware of the advantages of this coincidence.[3]

THE FUNCTION OF WAGES AFTER 1957

The limitations of wage structure were a major factor in the decision to develop direct controls over employment change. None the less, it is obvious that the ability of the Bureaux to expedite smooth intra-municipal employment transfers would be seriously affected by irrationality in local wage structures. To remedy this, the decentralisation gave local planning organisations more say in wage planning than had been the case in the First Five Year Plan.[4] What this

[1] The detailed control of internal movement in China was observed by the author in 1965–66. Apart from documentary checks, in many towns the railway stations are surrounded by barbed wire to prevent unauthorised access. It is probable that street level controls in the 1960s were equally stringent.

[2] In the case of Shanghai, pre-war data on the geographical origins of the population and labour force show that most migrants came from the adjacent areas. In 1932, for example, 67% of the population of Greater Shanghai were either born in Shanghai or Kiangsu Province, *Statistics of Shanghai compiled in 1933* (1933), p. 4. Mobility into Shanghai, moreover, was probably exceptional since data for Wusih and Nanking suggest that the pre-war labour markets in those cities were even more localised. Fang Fu-an, 'Shanghai labour', *Chinese economic journal*, August 1930, p. 871.

[3] For example the timing of the reforms was close. The population registration regulations were dated 9 January 1958 and the first extension of the Shanghai Municipality was made in the same month, HHPYK 1958 No. 3, pp. 46–9; Morris B. Ullman, p. 43. See also, 'Adjust administrative area plans: implement the system of workers alternating between agricultural and industrial work', *LT* 1958 No. 24, pp. 4–5.

[4] Wang Kuei-wu, CHCC 1958 No. 9, pp. 13–15.

meant in practice it is difficult to know, for in 1957 some Labour Bureau chiefs were openly sceptical about the willingness of centrally controlled enterprises to allow them any real role in wage determination.[1] But in the event, the reform was a step in the right direction.

EXPERIMENTS IN DECENTRALISATION

Between the initial reform of 1957 and the mid-1960s, the precise location of powers over hiring varied. These variations were partly regional, but they also reflected the ebb and flow of pressures from the centre – pressures that reflected the endless search for the optimum degree of decentralisation. For although the case for decentralisation was strong, some motives for reform were less rational than others, and these led to extremes of decentralisation that required more low-level skilled administrators than were available and put too much reliance on internal and Party controls.

Thus at first, in late 1957, it was the provincial and municipal authorities who were the beneficiaries of decentralisation. Then in the Great Leap Forward, the decentralisation was radicalised, so that effective powers over hiring and firing seem to have reverted to the enterprise and even to components of the enterprise such as the shop. The only external coordination at this time was of a loose variety exercised by *ad hoc* labour allocation organisations set up under Party inspiration and leadership. Apart from these, the Government was almost entirely dependent on the efficacy of internalised, ideological controls to ensure that labour administration at the enterprise level did not get out of hand.

In the aftermath of the Great Leap, however, it was seen that reliance on ideological, Party and *ad hoc* administrative controls was an inadequate safeguard against the evils of excessive hiring – particularly when, as in 1958, enterprises and organisations were actively encouraged to ignore financial constraints. Thus in 1961, the Minister of Labour formally announced that the Municipality was again to be the lowest planning level with authority over permanent

[1] *LT* 1957 No. 12, pp. 2–3 and 13.

hiring, and in 1962 it was openly admitted that, 'by the beginning of the Second Five Year Plan period an excessive *hsia fang* of hiring powers had taken place'.[1]

Thereafter, hiring controls seem to have been of three types: (1) municipal level control over permanent hiring;[2] (2) municipal level control over temporary hiring by industrial enterprises which took the form of flexible targets in enterprise labour plans (i.e. the number of temporaries to be employed had to be restricted to previously agreed limits);[3] and (3) street level control over casual employment in traditional occupations and small-scale relief and public works – probably under supervision of the district level Labour Office.[4]

This system has a strong appearance of rationality. It offers safeguards against hiring that would be reflected in the excessive and irreversible growth of the wage bill, while retaining the flexibility necessary to handle the problems of seasonal and casual employment. It seems unlikely, however, that escape from the dilemmas and patterns of behaviour of the 1950s has been complete. For the evidence of the earlier period shows that the imposition of formalised controls was always difficult in the face of an environment subject to enormous regional variations and of what appears to be a built-in preference for organisation through informal personal relationships.[5] Thus although the improved design of employment administration after 1957 must have made formal control more meaningful than before, it cannot have completely eliminated traditional and irregular employment practices. Also, oscillations in the intensity of the effort to control hiring seem bound to continue, until the time comes when job finding procedures are so efficient that there is no incompatibility between the objectives of maintaining control and minimising urban unemployment.

[1] Based on materials in *LT* 1958 No. 23, p. 5; *LT* 1959 No. 7, p. 12; *LT* 1962 No. 13, p. 2; *LT* 1963 No. 4; Ma Wen-jui, 'Problems of labour power in our country's socialist construction', *HHPYK* 1961 No. 3, pp. 100–6.

[2] Ma Wen-jui, speech cited above.

[3] 'Some problems in the control of temporary workers', *LT* 1963 No. 10, p. 31.

[4] 'Introducing a street level miscellaneous repair centre', *LT* 1962 No. 2, p. 18.

[5] The phrase 'yung szu jen kuan hsi' ('use private connections') occurs frequently in descriptions of evasions of official employment procedures in the 1950s. The 1947 Shanghai survey reported that only 4% of the factory labour had been recruited by formal methods, *Shang hai kung ch'ang lao kung t'ung chi*, p. 163.

Finally, there is the problem of the innate tendency of bureaucratic employment to expand. The Chinese called this 'unproductive' employment and included in the concept personnel in administrative organisations and non-technical staff in enterprises. As we have seen, although this type of employment was periodically attacked and reduced, its buoyancy seems irrepressible. To some extent, criticisms of the growth of bureaucratic employment in China seem irrational, since political control, industrial growth and urbanisation are all major policy goals that require rapid expansion of this type of employment.[1] The planned society must after all have its planners. Nonetheless, qualitative evidence suggests that the growth of bureaucratic employment was excessive and that its control presented real problems. The crucial issue was how to identify criteria that could be used to indicate where non-productive personnel were necessary – and in the 1960s the Bureaux established special departments whose task was to assist in the design of detailed schemes of work differentiation, which, when applied to an organisation of specified functions, could be used to determine the minimum complement of 'non-productives'.[2] The character of the *hsia fangs* in the 1960s, however, suggests that the efficacy of these campaigns was not great; and it may be argued that the nature of multi-tiered organisations and the lack of financial control intrinsic to socialist organisation, make the problem to some extent insoluble.[3]

THE LABOUR BUREAUX IN PERSPECTIVE

We have shown in this book that employment administration involved many agencies and organisations, but throughout our analysis we have tried particularly hard to understand the work of the Labour Bureaux. Looking back over the whole period, the evolution of the Bureaux can be seen to have had specific and interesting characteristics. First, from the Shanghai evidence, it

[1] Anthony Downs, *Inside bureaucracy* (1967), chapter XXI.
[2] *LT* 1958 No. 3, p. 2; *LT* 1962 No. 2, p. 21; *LT* 1962 No. 5, p. 11.
[3] Although the mechanics and forms differ, bureaucratic employment creation is not restricted either to socialist or low income countries. For example, a recent report has claimed that there are 9,000 functionless bureaucratic organisations in Italy – including an ineffective agency for liquidating other agencies. 'Scandal of useless jobs', *Sunday Telegraph* (London), 24 May 1970.

seems that the Bureaux' organisation, policies and even policy cycles had some continuity with the pre-1949 period. Thus in employment work, 1949 was a less important watershed than might have been supposed.

Secondly, for most of the period up to 1957, the Bureaux lacked the authority, clarity of purpose and resources necessary for consistent and effective action. This is seen in the failure to handle unemployment administration; and between 1953 and 1956, in the lack of implemented national labour plans. This weakness had two results. First, whenever some aspect of the Bureaux' work was regarded as exceptionally important – as for example the unemployment registration of 1952 – the Government ensured that the necessary resources were made temporarily available by involving in short campaigns the Party, the Youth League, the Unions and other sources of personnel and power. When, however, the Government did not come to the rescue, the Bureaux responded to insoluble problems by redefining their tasks so as to avoid them. Thus in 1954–55 they dropped unemployment work; in 1956 they abandoned hiring controls; and in early 1957 they attempted to evade responsibility for establishing small-scale enterprises to be manned by the unemployed.

One thing that the Bureaux did not appear to do was react to intolerable frustrations by producing schemes for utopian change – and this suggests that utopianism in the 1950s was generated outside rather than within the main administrative systems.

By mid-1957 the political leadership had become aware that effective labour administration was a prerequisite for other forms of planning and resource control. As a result, the Bureaux obtained some of the clarification of purpose and power they needed. This was momentarily obscured in the Great Leap Forward, but the Bureaux seem to have emerged again in the 1960s. The collapse of 1958 may well have been a result of the *hsia fang* movement, since this led to sharp reductions in the numbers employed in labour, as in all forms of administration.[1] By the 1960s, however, the flow of graduates from the Peking school for labour cadres must have increased the ability of the Bureaux to satisfy the demands made of

[1] *LT* 1958 No. 1, p. 13; *LT* 1958 No. 9, p. 30.

them, and thus have served to assure them of a permanent place in China's economic organisation.

EMPLOYMENT AND ECONOMIC STRATEGY

In our earlier chapters we tried to show how even the minutiae of employment administration were often related to wider issues of economic planning and policy. These links are found throughout the 1950s, although in the earlier years they formed only a subterranean background to more dramatic issues and decisions. In 1957 and 1958 they came to the surface and we can see how labour issues played an important part in the policy reformulations of this period.

In retrospect we can see that China, with a large and growing population, low land–man ratios, and a shortage of all forms of capital, was faced with an employment absorption problem of formidable proportions. Yet as we showed, in its early years the Government was confident that unemployment was a temporary phenomenon that could be eliminated by an acceleration of industrialisation and the development of socialist institutions. At this time the experience of the Soviet industrialisation process was very much in the minds of the Chinese planners. In Russia, the First Five Year Plan had transformed the unemployment of the New Economic Policy period into a labour shortage so acute that the transfer of manpower to the urban sector had to be forcible. The expectation was that a comparable sectoral transfer would take place in China and the communication of this idea to the rural population was a major factor in the huge, and in the event unwarranted, population migrations in the 1950s. The realisation that urban unemployment could not be solved by any feasible industrial growth rate, and that further institutional change could at best ameliorate the problem, led to a major revision of economic strategy.

At the simplest level, awareness of the problem was induced by the aggregate estimates of the supply and demand for labour during the Second and Third Five Year Plans. On the supply side, the growth of the urban labour force in the First Plan was seen to have been excessive and the situation was bound to deteriorate, since by the mid-1960s the size of the labour force would be accelerating in response to population growth in the 1950s. On the demand side the prospect was that no acceleration would be possible without abandonment of the overall strategy of the First and Second Plans.

Going a little deeper, we can see that in specific cities the prospects varied. In Shanghai and other cities in which labour and productivity rather than capital had been the main sources of growth, decelleration was bound to occur as the technical possibilities for increasing the labour–capital ratio were exhausted. In the key-point cities on the other hand, self-sustained growth would continue, but employment expansion would be limited by reliance on capital-intensive methods and by the growth of productivity that could be expected as the raw recruits absorbed in the early years of industrialisation reached new levels of skill and commitment.

The immediate response to these problems was the Great Leap Forward and the Commune movement which promised to provide the institutional changes necessary for massive labour absorption in agriculture and the expansion of urban employment as well. But these movements collapsed, partly because they were based on inaccurate estimates of the resources available for mobilisation, and partly because of a utopian optimism about the speed with which institutional change and political education could be expected to transform human thinking and behaviour.

In the years following this, the strategy for industrialisation seems to have followed the lines laid down in the Second Plan. This envisaged basic continuity with the First Plan, combined with increased emphasis on employment absorption as a criterion for investment, continuous urban out-migration and a much greater flexibility in planning, which in effect has reduced the plan period to one year.

EMPLOYMENT AND URBAN PLANNING

The reformulation of economic strategy just described related population, employment and industrialisation to the design of urban policy; for by the late 1950s, the Chinese planners had learned important lessons about the relationships between these variables. One lesson was that rapid shifts in the distribution of urban population and economic activity were both difficult and economically undesirable. This may have been related to the entrenched political power of the older cities, and was certainly a reflection of the partial immobility of the technical and organisational skills possessed by the populations of cities such as Shanghai. This immobility can be directly related to the failure to readjust inter-city real income differentials in a way that facilitated migration; it was also a reflection of the complementarities between these skills and their environment that made transfer without loss of productivity impossible.

The most obvious manifestation of the inefficiency of rapid shifts of inter-city economic power, was the excess production capacity in the older cities evident in 1954–55. But this was not all, for in the new cities total production costs (i.e. direct production costs plus overhead urban costs) were inflated by lack of scale and complementarities in the production and service sectors and by high transport costs. Thus although some aspects of the long-term case for a reduction of the urban concentration on the eastern seaboard remained valid, the planners became aware that the costs of such reduction were higher than anticipated and positively related to the speed with which it occurred. For these reasons, the Second Five Year Plan confirmed that the seaboard cities would be allocated resources to enable them to operate at full capacity and to expand to the extent allowed by the size of their existing infrastructure.[1]

There remained the problem of fluctuations in the urban economy. These were important because however employment administration was reorganised, it would be unlikely to withstand the strains of really violent fluctuations. Earlier, we argued that fluctuations in the 1950s were related to agriculture, the private sector and the adoption of unrealistic target rates of growth. By 1958 the modern private sector had disappeared, and in recent years policy measures must have diminished the importance of fluctuations of the kind experienced in the First Plan. A flexible foreign trade policy, for example,

[1] See Chou En-lai's report on the Second Five Year Plan, *HHPYK* 1956 No. 20, pp. 41–2.

has allowed fluctuations in imports to offset fluctuations in the supply of inputs from domestic agriculture, and the abandonment of publicised economic plans has meant that even if excessive optimism about China's economic potential has remained – failure to fulfil plans has involved no serious loss of face and no pressure therefore to ensure plan fulfilment by desperate and destabilising remedies.

In addition, we must remember that during the First and Second Plan periods some of the older cities were acquiring more diversified industrial bases, which must have meant that the instability of individual industries has become less important;[1] while in the keypoint cities increasing maturity should have been accompanied by a decline in the relative importance of the construction industry – probably the most unstable industry of all – and, in the longer run, randomisation of the age of the capital stock must lessen any tendency towards replacement cycles.

All these considerations lead us to think that urban economic performance between 1961 and 1966 was probably more stable than that of the 1950s, and if this was so, the effectiveness of economic planning and employment administration must have been enhanced.

CONCLUSION

Without more data, we cannot pursue our analysis of employment administration and urban economic development since 1958 any further. But the earlier period offers firmer ground for generalisation, and our main conclusions are that in the late 1950s the Chinese correctly saw that the maintenance of adequate levels of urban employment involved fundamental thinking about both the structure of economic administration and the size and functions of cities; and

[1] In Shanghai, two forces were at work in diminishing fluctuations by reducing dependency on agriculture. One was the growth in importance of heavy industry and the other was the diminishing dependence of light industry on agriculture. Between 1949 and 1957 the share of light and textile industries in total industrial output declined from 90% to 66%, and this trend was planned to continue in the Second Five Year Plan. Within light industry it was reported that direct and indirect dependence on agricultural materials fell from 63·9% to 39·52% between 1957 and 1962. *CFJP* 29 Sep. 1957; *CFJP* 27 Jul. 1956; *Ching chi yen chiou* (Economic Research) 1963 No. 11, p. 13.

that seen in perspective, employment administration is an impressive manifestation of China's capacity for imaginative institutional innovation. This capacity has been a crucial factor in the struggle for economic progress so far, but if the strains of population growth are to be contained, it may have to meet even severer tests in future.

APPENDIX

	(000's)
Total employment	2,418[a]
Industry, total	899[b]
of which: modern factory	(770)
workshop	(129)
Handicrafts, total	258[c]
of which: peripatetic and household	(38)
workshops employing fewer than ten men	(71)
individual handicraftsmen and others	(149)
Other small scale production	30[d]
Construction	30[e]
Transport and communication, total	177[f]
of which: the modern public system	(57)
pedicabs	(40)
carts	(80)
Stevedores	33[g]
Commerce, total	533[h]
of which: old private sector stores (pre-1956)	(221)
pedlars	(240)
old public sector commerce system	(72)
Food and services	50[i]
Education	72[j]
Health	30[k]
Banking	25[l]
Government, mass organisations and other	281[m]

SOURCES AND METHODS

[a] The number in employment at the end of 1956 was reported as 2,390,000 (*NCNA* 17 Aug. 1957). To obtain a figure for 1957 we add 110,000 for additional employment created in that year and deduct 82,000 for jobs estimated to have been lost in that year. The latter is made up of: (i) an estimated halving of the construction work force. (ii) 6,000 jobs that disappeared when cadres were sent to the countryside. (iii) 46,000 jobs